Acclaim for *The Power of Nunchi*

"Profoundly wise . . . This wonderful exploration of a nuanced Korean philosophy will appeal to any reader looking to hone skills of emotional perception."   —*Publishers Weekly*

"Nunchi is the Korean superpower you need now."
                                                    —*Evening Standard*

"A more profound way of looking at life than hygge or Marie Kondo's obsession with tidying sock drawers . . . It should be read by all politicians . . . and by those struggling in fractious relationships, or families squabbling on holiday. . . . We could all help ourselves by practicing the ancient art of nunchi."
                                                    —*The Times* (London)

"Essential reading . . . It's the golden buzzer—a simple, but life-changing, book for society. If we all had a little more nunchi, the world would be a better place."
                                                    —*Sunday Independent* (Ireland)

"In her practical and care-full guide, Euny Hong shows us how nunchi—the beautiful, still practice of mindfully reading people—can help us to live a more considered life in our distracted, digitally disconnected culture. *The Power of Nunchi* is the self-help bible we need."
          —Sarah Wilson, *New York Times* bestselling author of
          First, We Make the Beast Beautiful

"Euny Hong just taught me what I really want to be when I grow up: a nunchi ninja!"
                    —Zoe Chance, Yale School of Management

THE POWER OF NUNCHI

The Korean Secret to Happiness and Success

Euny Hong

PENGUIN BOOKS

PENGUIN BOOKS
An imprint of Penguin Random House LLC
penguinrandomhouse.com

First published in Great Britain by Hutchinson,
an imprint of Penguin Random House UK, 2019
Published in Penguin Books 2019

Library of Congress Cataloging-in-Publication Control Number: 2019023520
ISBN 9780143134466 (hardcover)
ISBN 9780525506263 (ebook)

Printed in Canada
1 3 5 7 9 10 8 6 4 2

Set in Chaparral Pro

All names and identifying characteristics have been changed
to protect the privacy of the individuals involved.

The world is full of obvious things which nobody by any chance ever observes.

The Hound of the Baskervilles, *Arthur Conan Doyle*

Contents

THE POWER OF NUNCHI

CHAPTER 1

What Is Nunchi?

Nunchi (noon-chee): "eye-measure," or the subtle art of gauging other people's thoughts and feelings to build harmony, trust, and connection.

Let's imagine you have just started a new job at a big company, and you're invited to a party where you want to make a great impression. When you walk into the room, everyone is laughing a bit too hard at the not-particularly-funny joke of an older woman you've never seen before. Do you:

A) Step in with a *really* funny joke, definitely much better than the one you just heard. Your new colleagues are going to love this!

B) Laugh along with the others, even though it's not very amusing.

C) Find a tactful moment to introduce yourself to the older woman, who you've correctly assumed must be the head of the company.

If you chose A, you seriously need to work on your nunchi. If you chose B, good work, you read the room correctly and picked up the right cues from your new colleagues. If you chose C, congratulations, you're already on your way to mastering the power of nunchi.

Nunchi is the Korean superpower. Some people even go so far as to say it's how Korean people can read minds— though there's nothing supernatural about it. Nunchi is the art of instantly understanding what people are thinking and feeling, in order to improve your relationships in life. Having great nunchi means continuously recalibrating your assumptions based on any new word, gesture, or facial expression, so that you are always present and aware. Speed is paramount to nunchi; in fact, if someone is highly skilled at nunchi, Koreans don't say they have "good" nunchi, they say they have "quick" nunchi.

In the short term, nunchi will save you from social embarrassment—you can't make a faux pas if you've read the room correctly. In the long term, nunchi will make the waters part for you. People will open doors that you never even knew existed. Nunchi will help you live your best life.

There's an old Korean expression about the power of nunchi: "If you have quick nunchi, you can eat shrimp in a monastery." Admittedly, this makes no sense until you understand that traditional Korean Buddhist monasteries are strictly vegetarian. In other words, the laws bend to your will.

Everyone can improve their lot by honing their nunchi; you don't have to be privileged, know the right people, or have an impressive academic pedigree. In fact, Koreans refer to nunchi as "the advantage of the underdog" for just those reasons. It's your secret weapon, even if you've got nothing else. As for those who were born with a silver spoon in their mouth, well, there is no faster way to lose your advantages in life than a lack of nunchi.

As Koreans say, "Half of public life is about nunchi." A well-honed and quick nunchi can help you choose the right partner in life or business, it can help you shine at work, it can protect you against those who mean you harm, and it can even reduce social anxiety. It can make people take your side even when they aren't sure why. Conversely, a lack of nunchi can make people dislike you in a way that is as mysterious to them as it is to you.

So if you're thinking, "Oh dear, not another Eastern fad—I've already thrown away half my clothes thanks to Marie Kondo," first of all, it's not a fad. Koreans have been using nunchi to evade or overcome more than 5,000 years' worth of slings and arrows.

You need only look to recent Korean history to see nunchi at work: the country went from Third World to First

World in just half a century. Only seventy years ago, after the Korean War, South Korea was one of the world's poorest nations—poorer than most of sub-Saharan Africa. To make matters worse, it had no natural resources at all: not a drop of oil, not an ounce of copper. By the twenty-first century, South Korea had become one of the richest, coolest, and most technologically advanced nations on the planet.

It now manufactures most of the world's semiconductors and smartphones. It is the only member nation of the Organisation for Economic Co-operation and Development (OECD) that started out as a borrower of money and then became a *lender* of money.[1]

Sure, some of that was down to the usual luck, hard work, and a little help from their friends, but if it were that simple, any number of other developing nations could have achieved exactly the same thing. Yet none did. The Korean economic miracle has always been based on nunchi: the ability to "eye-measure" other nations' rapidly evolving needs, to manufacture export products that evolve as quickly as those needs, and to recalibrate plans based on the universe's only constant—change.

If you still question the value of nunchi, ask yourself why K-pop is even a thing.

Nunchi is woven throughout all aspects of Korean society. Korean parents teach their children about the importance of nunchi from a very young age, on par with lessons such as "Look both ways before crossing the street" and "Don't hit your sister." "Why do you have no nunchi?!" is a common parental chastisement. As a child, I remember having accidentally offended a family friend, and defending myself to my father by saying, "I didn't mean to upset Jinny's mother." To which my father replied, "The fact that the harm wasn't intentional doesn't make it better. It makes it worse."

Some Westerners might find my dad's criticism difficult to understand. What parent would prefer that their child be mean deliberately rather than accidentally? But think of it another way: children who choose to be mean at least know what they hope to achieve by it, whether that's getting even with a sibling or winding up a parent. But a child who doesn't even know what consequences their words have on people? A child with no nunchi? No matter how sweet and kind they are, they are likely to be on the losing end of life, unless this cluelessness is trained out of them.

Some are born with nunchi, some achieve nunchi, and some have nunchi thrust upon them. I had it thrust upon me. When I was twelve years old, my family moved from the U.S. to South Korea. I didn't speak the language at all, yet I was enrolled in a Korean public school. This was the best nunchi crash course I could have had, because I had to assimilate into a foreign culture with zero linguistic clues. In order to work out what was happening in my new country, I had to be hyperreliant on my nunchi, which became my sixth sense.

What made it even more challenging was the huge nunchi gap between the U.S. and Korea. In the U.S., interactions are informal, and you can get by with minimal nunchi. Americans don't bow to each other; the language doesn't have a "polite" versus "familiar" hierarchy; and you can call grown-ups by their first names. By contrast, the Korean culture and language are hierarchical and full of more rules than there are stars in the sky. For example, Koreans cannot even call their own older siblings by their first names; it has to be an honorific such as "older brother" or "older sister." According to Confucian principles, a harmonious society requires everyone to know their place and act accordingly. Problem: if I didn't even know what to call my own siblings any more, I was 100 times more clueless as to how to behave in a Korean school.

I had no lever to pull except for watching what the other schoolkids were doing. That's how I learned two cardinal rules of nunchi: 1) if everyone is doing the same thing, there is always a reason. I had no idea how to stand at attention, or at ease; all I knew was that everyone else was doing it, so I studied their bodies closely and mimicked what they did;

2) if you wait long enough, most of your questions will be answered without your having to say a word. Which was great, because I didn't know any words.

This nunchi trial by fire helped me understand what was expected of me, it opened my mind up to love learning, and it also made the teachers and students more patient with me. Just over a year after arriving in Korea, I was first in my class and a prize-winning math and physics student. Within eighteen months, I was elected class vice president and was given the authority to hit other students (a slightly dubious privilege given to the favored few). All of this, despite the fact that my Korean was still terrible, and I still got made fun of for my Western ways. But I am living proof that you don't have to be the best in order to win—as long as you have quick nunchi.

Yes, I was a hard worker, but studying alone wouldn't have got me far without nunchi. Nunchi is what can turn a huge handicap (in my case, no knowledge of Korean) into an unexpected advantage: because the teachers were always talking too fast for me to follow their words properly or take many notes, I had to discern from the teachers' faces and tones of voice when they were saying something really important, as in they were probably going to include that topic in the exams. Loud voice, I learned = you will be tested on this. I also noticed, for example, that my seventh-grade physics teacher would hit her palm gently with a stick when she was trying to drive a point home. (Teachers carried sticks at all times; they were wooden bits of hardware covered with electrical tape. Usually they were for beating students.) So even though I was still a dunce and could barely take notes, the teachers were "telling" us what was going to be included in the exam without actually telling us.

Nunchi is a part of daily life in Korea, because Korean culture is what is known as "high context," which is to say that a great deal of communication is based not on words, but on the overall context, which has countless factors: body language, facial expressions, tradition, who else is present, and even silence. In Korea, what is *not* being said is every bit as important as the words that are spoken, and a person who pays attention merely to the words is getting just half the story. But this in no way means that you need nunchi only in Korea. Even in the West, life is full of high-context scenarios requiring your nunchi—even if you didn't know such a word existed.

You Need Nunchi

You have surely noticed that the more important a situation is, the greater the likelihood that the most crucial information is not expressed out loud, or not expressed truthfully. Nunchi might be your only ally in such moments.

When it comes to the practical application of nunchi in daily life, it's important to understand that the unit of nunchi is the room. What I mean by this is that the object of your observation should not be an individual, but should be the room as a whole and how the individuals within it are acting and reacting.

Have you ever been in a room when a famous person walks in? Even if your back is to the door, and you can't see who it is, you know from the reactions of everyone around you that something has changed. That is nunchi in action: an awareness of the cues we get from others.

You may not think of a room as a single living, breathing organism, but it is. It has its own "temperature," "barometric pressure," volume, mood—and these are in constant flux. Koreans talk of a room as having a *boonwigi*— the room's atmosphere or wellness level, so to speak. Everyone is a contributing member of this boonwigi just by being there. Act with no nunchi, and you ruin the boonwigi for the whole room. Act with great, or "quick," nunchi, and you can enhance the atmosphere of the room for everyone.

It may help to think of a room as a beehive. Even if everyone seems to be acting independently, a part of their brain is contributing to the hive mind. Everyone has a role. Including you. Your job? To work out what your role is.

Until you discover your role—and even after you do—you should always be "eye-assessing": a fruitful activity with immediate benefits! You don't have to be anxious about doing or saying the right thing if you remember your primary activity is eye-assessment.

So what is it that you're observing? A skilled nunchi practitioner understands they are seeking answers to these two questions: "What is the emotional energy of this room?" and "What kind of emotional energy can I emit in order to flow with that?"

And why should you care about what vibes you are transmitting? It is best expressed in a saying often attributed to Maya Angelou: "I've learned that people will forget what you said, people will forget what you did, but people will never forget how you made them feel."

Here are some examples of poor nunchi. If you can recall similar incidents, think about the consequences you or others suffered as a result:

- You walk into a room and see people looking somber. You joke, "Where's the funeral?" only to discover that someone's father literally just died.
- Your boss is slamming doors and for some reason you hear people crying in the office toilets. That's the day you choose to ask your boss for a pay raise.

- You're at an "open house" for a prestigious company where you are angling to get a job. You spend the whole time trying to impress an employee because he has a flashy tie and acts important. Only later, when you get a text from him asking, "Care for dinner and a play?" do you discover that he was chatting you up. You also learn that the disheveled lot whom you'd assumed were interns were in fact the people running the company.

An intrinsic part of nunchi is the dimension of change: understand that everything is in flux. As the Greek philosopher Heraclitus wisely wrote in the sixth century BC, "You can't step into the same river twice." Adapting that principle to nunchi: the room you walked into ten minutes ago is not the same room as it is now. Being aware of your preconceptions, and learning how they can inhibit your powers of observation and adaptation, is a key part of honing your nunchi. Most of us understand that different situations require different behaviors—we don't act the same way at a funeral as we would at a birthday party—but sometimes the very familiarity of a situation can blind us to the fact that everything in it has changed, and so should we.

A successful businessperson understands the importance of adapting quickly to change. Some investment banks conduct interviews in which the interviewers start fussing with the windows or moving conference rooms midway through, precisely to see how the candidate deals with unexpected changes. Those who are unable to adapt to the unexpected are, in the interview and in life in general, at a disadvantage.

When you enter a room, having good nunchi means observing before you begin to speak or interact. Who is standing with whom? Who has three biscuits on their plate when everyone else has only taken one? We have powerful social instincts that give us strong clues about the room, but we have to be observant—more focused on others than on ourselves—in order to read them.

Sherlock Holmes, the Victorian-era detective conceived by author Sir Arthur Conan Doyle, was an expert in reading the room. From his very first meeting with his friend and sleuthing partner Dr. John Watson, Holmes is able to deduce that Watson has recently served as an army doctor in Afghanistan, based on his tan ("his face is dark, and that is not the natural tint of his skin, for his wrists are fair"), his haggard face, and the stiff way he holds his arm, denoting an old injury. Later in the stories he gently chastises Watson for his inability to do the same: "You see, but you do not observe."

Holmes is a master of using his observational skills to solve mysteries: a woman's dress has mud splashes only on the left sleeve, so Holmes can tell that the woman must have been sitting to the left of a driver in an uncovered horse-drawn vehicle. In several stories, he is able to gain clues by studying people's smoking habits, or the ash they leave behind.

We can't all be Sherlock Holmes, but we can learn to apply some of his skills in our everyday lives. And just like Sherlock Holmes, whose detections are made in a split second, speed is essential when it comes to nunchi. You must adapt rapidly to every new piece of information and every new person who enters the room.

Let's say you're being interviewed for a job by the department manager, Jack, who tells you, "The job is pretty autonomous. Would you say you're good at working solo? That's what we're looking for." As you are about to answer, in barges a woman introducing herself as Jill but giving no other information about herself. She says to you, "Hey, I have some questions too. This job will have you working closely with a team. Are you a team player? Because we're really not looking for a lone-wolf type." In other words, Jack and Jill have given contradictory descriptions of the job.

Do you say you're a lone wolf to appease Jack? Or do you say you're a team player to please Jill? You have to decide quickly. You can't go home and google her title. What you do notice, however, is that Jack is deferential to Jill and keeps his mouth shut while Jill is talking. Also, you note that she didn't apologize for lateness.

If you are in this situation, do you tell them:

A) "Well, Jack and Jill, you've both said totally contra-dictory things. Why don't you get your act together and call me then, ha-ha."

B) "I think I really shine as a lone wolf." Your reason-ing: Jack was the first one you met and therefore he's the decision maker. Jill didn't apologize for lateness; that's rude and I'm not listening to her. Plus she's female and thus probably Jack's assistant.

C) "Well, I'm equally good at working solo and also in groups. I'm simply good at everything."

D) "I can think of situations where I've done well both solo and in groups, but I think I really excel at cooperative work." Your thinking: that's what Jill said she wanted, and based on her comportment I think she is probably Jack's boss.

On the balance of probabilities, you are best going with option D. Jill didn't apologize for lateness because she doesn't care what Jack thinks. You would be reasonable to conclude that Jill is senior to Jack and it's Jill whom you have to impress. She's the decision maker.

Developing quick nunchi can help you get that job. It can win you more friends. It can make people take your side even when they aren't sure why. Great nunchi will smooth your path to success. Learning to develop your nunchi is something you can start to do immediately, right where you are, regardless of your education or your job or what you think your prospects are. You don't need to buy any fancy equipment to become a nunchi ninja, or take training courses. All you need is your eyes and your ears, and some guidance on how to use them wisely.

The popular epic book-and-television saga *Game of Thrones* could also be called *Game of Nunchi*: it juxtaposes characters with extremely quick nunchi against those with fatally bad nunchi. The character with the best nunchi by far is the "Halfman" Tyrion Lannister. His defining trait is that he can sense when threats are real and takes them seriously. Almost every other character in the series has bad nunchi, particularly the ones who don't care that winter is coming and who don't believe in the existence of the White Walkers— the withered, scary ice creatures—despite abundant proof that they're set to destroy mankind. The entire Stark family starts the series with awful nunchi—particularly Sansa, who ruins everyone's lives because she's a bad judge of character and wants to marry the sadistic Prince Joffrey. As the series progresses, and they're forced to rub shoulders

with the worst life has to offer, their nunchi improves...
slowly.

Don't be like the Starks. Improve your nunchi before
life forces you to do so, the hard way.

Practicing nunchi takes a lot of time and effort. But you
know what takes even more time and effort? Cleaning up
after you've made a bad impression. Dealing with the anxiety of not knowing why people are suddenly mad at you.
Unpoisoning a well you didn't even mean to poison.

This book will show you that nunchi isn't some quaint
Korean custom like taking off your shoes before entering a
house. Nunchi is the currency of life.

CHAPTER 2

The Korean Superpower

Korea, some claim, has been invaded 800 times in its history. Why? It's on the nexus of both China and Japan and, as any historian will tell you, it's a curse for a small country to be in such a strategic location.

Yet despite this tumultuous history, Koreans have not just survived as a nation, but thrived. As well as its astonishing pauper-to-prince economic trajectory, Korea has become a cultural dynamo that punches above its weight globally.

According to the concert ticket seller StubHub, America's third-highest ticket-selling act of fall 2018 (after Elton John and Ed Sheeran at one and two) was the K-pop boy band BTS.

There is no earthly reason why this should be happening. These songs aren't even in English; in fact, they're in a language that is spoken *in only two countries in the world*: North and South Korea.

Nor is it rational that Korean beauty products have become globally mainstream, and available in major retail chains from Paris to New York. Korean cosmetics are not revolutionarily different from other beauty products, yet they have presented themselves as so cutting edge, so modern, that K-beauty is a recognized influence around the world.

So how does a country that had almost no indoor plumbing just seventy years ago become almost mythically cool?

Nunchi, obviously. Survival of the fittest, to paraphrase Mr. Darwin, doesn't mean survival of the strongest; it means survival of those with the quickest nunchi.

Where Did Koreans Get Their Nunchi?

Korea's folk tales celebrate nunchi, and the most famous one of all is about the legendary hero Hong Gildong (Hong is the surname; no relation to me), a sixteenth-century Korean Robin Hood. Little is known about the real man, but in traditional lore, Hong used his nunchi to avoid an assassination attempt, overthrow a king, and become king in his place.

Every folk story ever told is basically about the triumph of nunchi over adversity. The tale of Hong Gildong is no exception.

Hong was born to a king's concubine (and a low-ranking one at that), and thus was never treated as a legitimate son, despite being the king's favorite. Due to jealousy from the Head Concubine, Hong is forced to leave the palace and has to live by his wits...in other words, his nunchi. Hong's nunchi allows him to see the proverbial writing on the wall: that he'd better leave home or he'll be assassinated. It's what allows him to adapt like a chameleon to any situation and act in whatever way is most likely to be effective within that particular situation, such as posing as a government inspector when he wants to be noticed, or a rickshaw driver when he wants to be ignored.

To learn more about Hong and his nunchi, I spoke to Minsoo Kang, a Korean professor of European history at the University of Missouri–St. Louis, who did the first comprehensive English translation of *The Story of Hong Gildong*.[2] In addition to being a scholar, Kang is also one of the first people who leaped to mind when I was trying to think of people I knew who had excellent nunchi.

Kang explained why Hong, or anyone in traditional Korean society (particularly an illegitimate son), would need nunchi: in a rigid and complicated class system (even the classes have classes within them!), nunchi is a necessity.

"In the Joseon era [which ran from the late fourteenth to the late nineteenth century], multigenerational families lived together in this massive compound," notes Kang. "Even among the women, it got complicated with a hierarchy of several concubines. It got extremely complicated when there were multiple kids. If you lived in that environment, you had to develop nunchi in order to survive."

To provide some context for Kang's observation, it may help to mention that premodern Korea had three major religions. These are, in order of adoption:

Animism: the belief that all entities have souls, especially mountains. A Western analog might be Druidism, the religion that brought us Stonehenge, as practiced by ancient Celtic cultures.

Confucianism: the official state philosophy in the Joseon era, which emphasizes order in society and a hierarchy in which all know their place.

Buddhism: the hardest to define of the three, but based partly on acceptance that life is full of suffering, and the way to achieve inner peace in such a world is a life of contemplation and an awareness of the far-reaching consequences of your actions—be that littering or being cruel to animals or people.

Though Confucianism is the belief system most relevant to Hong Gildong's story, all three religions gave rise to the Korean emphasis on quiet contemplation and an awareness of how your actions can have an impact on your environment.

Kang has keen insight into why Koreans value nunchi so much: "A lot of it comes from the fact that Korea has been invaded so many times," he said. "Korea was too small to actually fight back, so they had to accommodate these waves of invaders, one after another. How could they deal with these new people coming in—the Mongols, the Manchus, the Japanese? Koreans had no choice but to develop these methods of nunchi."

If it weren't for nunchi, Korean culture would no longer exist. During the Japanese colonization of Korea, from 1919 to 1945, the Korean language and culture were in the process of being phased out. Korean families were given Japanese surnames, for example.

"Had the Japanese won World War II," Kang observed, "their plan was to annihilate the Korean language and culture entirely." In order to preserve any Koreanness, Kang notes, the nation had to go into nunchi overdrive.

They had to walk the tightrope of placating their Japanese overlords, while also finding the right approach and timing to preserve Korean newspapers, non-Shinto religions, and Korean instruction in schools.

Kang also explained the role nunchi played in South Korea's rags-to-riches economic miracle, particularly at the hands of longtime dictator President Park Jung-hee (Park is the surname), who served as president from 1961 to his assassination in 1979. Kang explained, "As much as I despise Park, he saw that the only way South Korea was going to become prosperous was to get out there into the world, to send people to other countries to learn English and other skills, and create jobs for Korean people. The ability to read other people and other cultures was absolutely necessary." By contrast, says Kang, North Korea cut itself off entirely from the world, "which is why North Korea now has terrible nunchi."

How can we be sure Korean nunchi worked? For one thing, there are now 70 million Korean speakers; by all historical logic, there should arguably be zero.

In modern-day Korea, nunchi is as important as ever. Kang points out that in Korea, "Realpolitik is nunchi. The South Korean president has to use nunchi to figure out what to do both with the Americans and with North Korea." Indeed, after the historic 2018 handshake and noodle-slurping summit between South Korean president Moon Jae-in and North Korean premier Kim Jong-un, many Western journalists were confused as to the significance of what had happened. How was shaking hands and eating noodles going to bring about peace? What they did not understand was that this was a nunchi game of two Koreans against the rest of the world.

The goal of the two Korean leaders most likely didn't have much to do with reunification, as was widely assumed. Though it's hard to be sure, many experts believe that the meeting was meant as a defiant gesture to the U.S., Japan, and China: all the nations that were assuming they'd be micromanaging the relationship between the two Koreas.

If you study the videos of Moon and Kim together, you will note that they appear to be in carefully choreographed symmetry (though no one but the inner circle knows for certain whether this was preplanned). It's obvious that they are always basing their own movements on each other.

That's nunchi in action. From the first greeting, they were careful to show that neither was dominant nor subservient to the other. They bowed at an approximately equal angle and for an equal duration. When they hugged, they let go at the same time. When they were served the special lunch of North Korean buckwheat noodles, they both made a point to enjoy the meal but with unreadable, polite faces and at roughly the same pace. If one of them had slurped the noodles with gusto and sung the dish's praises while the other ate it slowly and grimacing, this could have been interpreted as a statement of how each of them felt about North Korea. The two were at all times apace with each other. This was a show of unity. The summit could have been about basketball or Hennessy cognac, for all anyone knows. The content of the talks mattered less than the overall show of strength and autonomy, while intentionally confusing other political players.

Nunchi is still interwoven in all aspects of modern Korean society. Westerners doing business in Korea for the first time are often bewildered to discover that during their first, second, or even third meeting with their Korean counterparts, the business at hand isn't directly discussed at all. In those first few meetings, Koreans are trying to work out whether you are trustworthy, in it for the long haul, and whether you see eye to eye with them—all of which has to be eye-measured.

After the historic June 2018 summit between U.S. president Donald Trump and North Korean premier Kim Jong-un, the Korean press went on a nunchi-under-the-microscope spree, analyzing the two leaders' gestures, body language, and other *seeming* minutiae. Numerous Korean media sources commented that the Kim–Trump handshake lasted twelve seconds—a happy medium between a short, casual shake and the awkwardly long nineteen-second handshake Trump had shared with Japanese prime minister Shinzo Abe. The Korean press also noted that, whereas Trump's handshake with certain leaders often resembled a tug-of-war—with each party subtly pulling the other's hand toward himself—Trump and Kim's handshake was at the exact center of the space between the two men, and the grip strength appeared to be equal. Very few people know for certain what was really said at that meeting, but optically the South Korean press interpreted the handshake as demonstrating that the U.S. and North Korea wanted to show that each country had the same amount to lose or gain from the other.

The Nunchi Scale

One Korean psychologist, Jaehong Heo, a professor of psychology at Kyungpook National University in the southeastern Korean city of Daegu, is attempting to use nunchi as a new template for treating psychiatric patients.

Heo has created an innovative "Nunchi Scale," a way to measure nunchi "objectively."[3] Similar scales have been in use for decades in the Western social sciences, to measure self-esteem, satisfaction with life, and the Empathy

Quotient, the last of which was developed by renowned Cambridge psychologist Simon Baron-Cohen.

Heo's team found that better nunchi can make people live happier lives: a high score on the Nunchi Scale correlated with high scores in self-esteem, satisfaction with life, and empathy. His long-term goal with this research is to come up with a way of treating Korean patients within a culturally specific context, by helping them improve their nunchi.

In one study, Heo and his team came up with a list of statements that in their view most exemplified nunchi. They then tested 180 university-age students on their nunchi.

The statements Heo's team came up with as a measure of an individual's nunchi included the following. Here, "yes" answers indicate high nunchi levels:

- I feel awkward saying something without knowing the other person's mood/mental state.
- Even if someone is saying something indirectly, I still comprehend the subtext.
- I am good at quickly discerning the other person's mood and inner state.
- I do not make other people uncomfortable.
- At a social gathering, I am able to distinguish easily between when it's time to leave and when it's not time to leave.

It is clear from Heo's research that those individuals who are attuned to the emotions of others, and who are able to read the room accurately, find that life is easier than it might be for those whose nunchi is lacking.

A few things are worth noting in the survey itself. First, the use of the word "quickly" in the third bullet point (and in several other questions not included here), which is in keeping with the notion of speed being important in nunchi (by contrast, the Empathy Quotient makes no note of speed). Second, "I do not make other people uncomfortable" isn't really an action—it's a non-action. Which gets to a really important point about nunchi: to borrow a line from the physician's Hippocratic Oath, you might say that a key nunchi principle to go by is "First, do no harm."

A medical doctor doesn't start immediately prescribing penicillin or chemotherapy as soon as a patient walks in. The doctor first makes a diagnosis and determines what treatment is necessary, if any. Before tackling the matter of fixing things, the doctor first makes sure that nothing they do causes active harm. Some people are fatally allergic to penicillin, for example, or their cancer is so far advanced that chemo will only serve to ruin their quality of life. Without a diagnosis, the so-called help is not helpful.

Nunchi dictates that we should all endeavor to "first, do no harm," but we often fail because our nunchi becomes hostage to our desire to fix things. Sometimes, well-meaning people try to "help" a situation but actually make it worse.

For example, when a nunchi-deficient person sees someone is crying, they may draw attention to the situation by bringing Kleenex and loudly asking if they are OK, instead of eye-assessing whether the person wants to be left alone.

Everyday Nunchi in Korea

In Korea, Japan, and other Asian nations, business cards are terribly important, even now. Even though Korea far outpaces the West in digital technology and social media, Korean business people still use paper cards. They wouldn't dream of telling a new business contact to look them up on LinkedIn.

Westerners stopped relying on business cards some time ago. At least two American companies put off printing my cards until a critical mass of employees needed them at once, because they wanted to benefit from a bulk discount at the printer. A Korean would gasp if you were to tell them this; it would be like your new boss telling you that there's no toilet paper in the office bathroom because they stock up only during the post-Christmas sale.

In Korea, business cards are a proxy for your identity. A job with no cards is not a job; a person with no cards is not a contributing member of society.

In Korea, if someone gives you their business card, it's an extension of their own body. They give it to you with two hands while bowing; you must also receive it with two hands while bowing. You look at the card and read it attentively for a few seconds. You don't put it in your back pocket, stuff it in your wallet, use it to takes notes on, or molest it in any other way. You put it away in a case made precisely for these cards.

None of this is convenient, which is the whole point. By making a big fuss and bother about something as trivial as a card, you are showing your counterparts that you value them over your own convenience.

An addiction to convenience is the enemy of nunchi.

Holding your sleeve

In Korea (as in many regions, from the Middle East to East Asia), when you go out drinking with others, you fill their glasses before filling your own. And when you pour, you use the nonpouring hand to hold the sleeve of your pouring hand. Traditionally, this was because Korean clothing had enormous drooping sleeves and no one wanted to dip these accidentally in the other person's drink. But why would Koreans persist with the tradition, when modern-day sleeves don't dangle? Even if they are wearing a T-shirt, why do they still grab their naked forearm? Because it's a way of closing the distance between yourself and others. You are demonstrating your respect for them by doing things in a deliberate fashion. You are also telegraphing to your *own* brain to be present in the moment and acknowledge the other person in front of you. Again, it's an act of nunchi over convenience.

Nunchi's worst enemy: the smartphone

If ever there were proof that we need nunchi now more than ever, it's the fact that people who walk while staring at their smartphones don't even notice a two-ton car approaching. Many people hardly notice if a driver yells at them to pay attention, because it seems as though society feels the driver's responsibility to notice that you're on the phone is equal to, or greater than, your responsibility to notice the oncoming car.

If staring at your smartphone prevents you from noticing something as massive as a moving car, smartphones will also prevent you from noticing such "minor" signs as what your own loved ones, your colleagues, or your boss are thinking or feeling. You might be at a bar tweeting "So happy! #OldFriendsRule" without realizing that your old friend is miserable.

It's so much easier to look at your phone than to observe what's happening around you. But it's not technology's fault; it's our fault for taking the easy way out rather than dealing with the discomfort of being around humans. To a nunchi ninja, the inability to deal with awkward silences is a weakness.

In fact, seeking out distraction has become such second nature that most people would practically have a nervous breakdown if there were a thirty-second lull in a conversation. It's gotten to the point where it's no longer considered rude to look at your phone in a social setting; in fact, it's rude to ask someone to put away their phone. Teachers I know who vowed never to allow their students to use phones in the classroom have all but capitulated.

Smartphones haven't been around for long enough to see what the long-term effects will be, but I guarantee that, all other things being equal, those who are able to put away their phones and read the room will get much further in life.

It's obvious to many of us that social media is not a good way to read people, which is why we compensate with ridiculous hyperbole such as saying that a picture was so impressive that it "broke the internet" or "blew everyone's mind." Ordinary descriptors that you could use face-to-face seem insufficient on social media, hence the inflated language.

To look at a small sample of how technology erodes nunchi: we all have that friend who is constantly hoodwinked by horrible people they meet online.

No matter how savvy you are with online interactions, you should give very little credence to what you learn through them. There is no substitute for in-person meetings, as you still need the unmediated, real-time reactions of people around you to know what they are thinking. You can't get what you want out of people as effectively if you can't read them, it's as simple as that.

So how do you overcome the corrosive effects that technology has on nunchi? You can take a few small steps that will make a big difference.

First of all, texting emotional messages never leads to a good place. Your first text is to the person, but all subsequent texts are to texts. It's just your phone communicating with another phone. Nothing ever got resolved that way.

Face-to-face communication is obviously best for a serious conversation. But if the person's not around and you have to resort to email, tack on these extra sentences at the end:

1. "So what do you think?"—because you care what they think, and you can't read their body language over email.
2. "Let's talk more when I see you"—in other words, take the conversation offline.

Then, *take action*: pull out your calendar and set up that face-to-face meeting.

Nunchi for Non-Koreans

You might be thinking, "I don't plan to go to Korea; how is nunchi useful to me?"

What makes you so sure that nunchi-style concepts are not useful in the West? Consider why some people conduct important business over golf and why most first dates involve dinner or another meal. Is it to save time by multitasking? No. We do it because of an implicit belief that you can tell a lot about people by the way they behave on a golf course or in a restaurant.

Nunchi is a form of emotional intelligence. Although the importance of emotional intelligence in everything from child-rearing to becoming a corporate superstar is now well understood, in practice many people still secretly pooh-pooh it. If only those people understood that entire civilizations were built on nunchi, they might be less skeptical of emotional intelligence.

Once upon a time, nunchi was a crucial part of classical Western philosophy and religion. It wasn't called nunchi, of course. But the values embodied by nunchi were there in ancient times. They were vitally important to the ancient Greek and Roman Stoics, such as Marcus Aurelius, who served as emperor of Rome from AD 161 to AD 180. In his *Meditations*, he wrote many pieces of nunchi-worthy advice, such as: "The first rule is to keep an untroubled spirit. The second is to look things in the face and know them for what they are."

The biblical book of Proverbs advises, "When there are many words, offense is unavoidable; but he who restrains his lips is wise."

Nunchi-esque principles were important to early Christians, too. Some, such as certain medieval Christian saints, referred to the similar concept of "discernment," or "discrimination." In fact, the seventh-century Eastern Orthodox Saint John of Damascus wrote that the virtue of discernment "is greater than any other virtue; and is the queen and crown of all the virtues."

According to Dom Alcuin Reid, a Benedictine prior in France who has written extensively on theology, "In a religious context, discernment is the process of removing your own desires and prejudices from a situation in order to determine what might be the will of God. The key to discernment is that all of the relevant factors have been considered dispassionately by the observer, before a decision is made. Just doing what you want is not discernment."

In reality it is very hard to overcome our inbuilt prejudices, but being aware of them at least allows us to ask whether we are acting out of self-interest or for the good of all. Whether you care about the will of God or not, we can all learn to view situations with distance and discernment.

These traditional Western beliefs dovetail perfectly with the concept of nunchi. In modern times, however, these tenets of stillness and discernment seem to have fallen by the wayside. The Western emphasis on "believing in yourself" and asserting your individuality is particularly instilled in young children. There's nothing wrong with confidence, but too much focus on the self can mean neglecting the social contract—our responsibility to others. It is possible to be true to ourselves and still treat others as we wish to be treated, instead of simply demanding that the world gives us the respect we think we deserve.

Concepts such as nunchi might be seen as politically incorrect in modern times, as they require you to make judgments on people based on very little concrete evidence. The problem here is that the vast majority of situations in life are lacking in concrete evidence and yet we still have to navigate our way through them. Nunchi can show you how to approach the world with discernment, not bias.

QUICK QUIZ

Which of the following statements represents quick nunchi?

A.   After a cup of tea, your host says, "I'm not sure I bought enough lamb, but would you like to stay for dinner?" You say, "Sure, I'll just eat the side dishes."

B.   At a work meeting, your colleague completes her presentation and says, "So if there are no more questions, I guess we can break for lunch." At that moment, you say, "*I* have a question, actually."

C.   You know your boss stress-eats chocolate bars when he's in a bad mood, so you glance in his trash can to see if there are any wrappers before asking for a promotion.

D.   You barge into a room and tell a joke.

Correct answer: C. In this scenario, you've paused a beat to "eye-measure" your boss's mood, thereby decreasing the likelihood of rejection.

Scenario A is a host's nightmare. They clearly don't want you to stay. If you are thinking, "Well, the hosts should have specifically asked me to leave if that was what they wanted," you're being obnoxious and pushing your value system on to another person. They're in their own home, dammit, and they are not obligated to choose directness over politeness just because you'd prefer it.

With B, the cue for you to keep quiet was "lunch."

As for D, unless the building is on fire, it is never a good idea to barge in to a room and say *anything* without first eye-measuring the room. For all you know, they could have been talking about the latest terror attack before you walked in. It's a good idea never to start any new conversation with a joke. No one will hate you for entering a situation without a joke.

CHAPTER 3

Nunchi Blockers

Any radical undertaking to live your best life requires you to examine a lifetime of cultural values that are getting in your way. Everyone is born with the potential for nunchi, but in order to draw it out, you have to challenge some of the received wisdom that has been thrown at you since birth; I call these cultural traits "nunchi blockers." Most people are unaware that they favor some traits over others, and that these might hinder their ability to read people and connect with them. Some of the biases of Western culture are these:

- Empathy is valued over understanding.
- Noise is valued over stillness and quiet.
- Extroversion is valued over introversion.
- Jagged edges are valued over roundness.
- Individualism is valued over collectivism.

Let's examine these preconceived values one by one and show how each of them is standing in your way of making your life better through nunchi. It's important to note that biases are often very hard to undo, but even just being aware of them will improve your nunchi.

Nunchi blocker 1:
Empathy is valued over understanding

The road to hell is paved with empathy.

Nunchi and empathy have some similarities: both traits aim to understand what the other person is thinking or feeling, with the ultimate aim of easing that person's suffering. One problem with the modern Western mind-set is an overemphasis on empathy. For some reason, empathy holds a kingly position among the virtues and is regarded as a be-all and end-all to understanding another person. While it's true that all decent human beings are marked by their capacity for empathy, it remains the case that, taken in isolation, empathy is overrated. Empathy can be selfish, and I would argue it does not always lead to understanding. It centers around the person feeling it. *Your* feelings.

Since empathy and nunchi are easily confused, I've drawn up some handy comparisons between nunchi and empathy below.

NUNCHI	EMPATHY
Sometimes requires putting up with some personal discomfort for the sake of others (nunchi and empathy have this in common)	Sometimes requires putting up with some personal discomfort for the sake of others
Focused on the room as a whole	Focused on the person you are talking to, or one uniform group of people (a certain minority group, a famine-stricken country, for example)
Sometimes silence is the best response	Speaking to the suffering party is usually expected
You observe while retaining mental distance	You attempt to plunge into the mind of the other person
Nunchi has no moral component	Empathy is "the right thing to do" from a societal and religious point of view
One can be emotionally neutral	Strong emotional component, which can lead to others taking advantage of you
Gender-neutral	Often thought of as a feminine trait
Speed is crucial	Speed plays no role

As you see, empathy and nunchi are quite different, though you need both in order to get along with people or simply to understand them. In my personal experience, as a teacher's-pet Asian female, empathy is a weapon that others have tried to turn against me. I'd say that when someone has chided me to "be more empathetic," about half the time it's because they were trying to shame me into being more docile. The other half of the time, they were trying to get me to lower my guard, so they could get something out of me.

Empathy without nunchi is like words without grammar or syntax—meaningless noise.

Have you ever tried to buy a carpet at a souk? It frequently involves the seller saying he has to feed his family. I mean, I understand you have to feed your family and I do have empathy for that, but if you can't support yourself with a 10,000 percent markup for a sweat-matted piece of cloth that last week was being used as a camel-saddle buffer, you are doing something wrong. You are barking up the wrong tree, my friend. I see your empathy and I raise you some nunchi.

These days one hears a lot about narcissists, sociopaths, and psychopaths. What they all share is a lack of empathy. However, it's possible to have *too much* empathy; it can lead you to fall victim to those same people.

If you are in an abusive domestic situation, for example, empathy is your enemy. Empathy can get you killed. Abusers are known to target empathetic people, because the latter are more likely to excuse poor behavior if the abuser was "tired" or "had a bad childhood." Nunchi, on the other hand, can help you recognize abuse before you are too far gone. It can save your life.

KOREAN VIEWS OF EMPATHY

Obviously, Koreans are not monsters; they value empathy as well as nunchi. Indeed, they have a proverb about the importance of empathy: "change location and think" (a Korean expression of Chinese origin, pronounced *yuk ji sa ji*). In other words, "look at things from a different point of view." The English equivalent would be something like "put yourself in someone else's shoes." But as you can immediately see, there is a fundamental difference between the Korean version and the English version.

The Korean expression "change location and think" simply means "move," or to put it in nunchi terms, "perch yourself in a different part of the room, like a cat."

The English expression "put yourself in someone else's shoes," however, means "try to pretend *you are the other person*."

I have always found this image revolting. Wearing other people's shoes is how you get athlete's foot. It's also a violation of personal boundaries; saying you can't understand someone until you've been in their shoes requires the kind of intimacy that no life lesson should require.

If you are in someone's shoes, you are compromising your own ability to see their problem—and the overall situation—objectively. To paraphrase a famous observation by the nineteenth-century French writer Guy de Maupassant, the Eiffel Tower is the only place in Paris where Paris is unrecognizable. When you are "embodying" someone, it's impossible to really see them objectively because you are far too close.

Let's say you summon all the empathy you have, and you come up short because you have not directly experienced what your counterpart has and cannot imagine yourself in that situation. What do you say, "Sorry, I got nothing"?

How are surgeons supposed to treat a patient if they completely inhabit the mind of a sick person? One of my best friends is a medical doctor. She won't let me be her patient. Why? Because her excessive empathy for me as a friend would prevent her from making an objective evaluation.

A real nunchi ninja can pick up another person's feelings whether they can "relate" to the person or not. Using your nunchi means that you can grasp what is happening even if you don't have anything in common with the other person—even if you don't speak the same language.

Nunchi blocker 2:
Noise is valued over stillness and quiet

In Western cultures we often discourage quiet contemplation, to the awful point that if someone is pausing to think before answering a question, we say, "Hello! Earth to Tom! Did you hear me?"

Nunchi is impossible for those with no ability to quiet their mind. The importance of silencing your thoughts may make more sense if you understand that nunchi isn't 100 percent cultural—it's largely biological. Nunchi is a way of honoring your five senses, your gut (which many modern gurus call the "second brain"), and your wiser, older, instinctive brain.

The brain can be divided roughly into three parts. The neocortex—which controls most of what we call rational thought—is, for primates, the largest part of the brain. It was the last part of the brain to develop evolutionarily, and it is the slowest to develop over the course of your life. So in other words, it's the youngest part of the brain but it thinks it's the smartest.

The second-oldest part of the brain is the limbic brain, which all mammals have; this controls emotions. The oldest is the reptilian brain, which governs instinct and survival. The "Nunchi Brain" (so to speak) requires all three parts of the brain—neocortex, limbic, and reptilian—with a de-emphasis on the neocortex.

In modern Western life, we value the giant neocortex above all. And it makes sense, since we wouldn't be human without the neocortex. But it makes a lot of noise, drowning out important messages offered by other parts of the brain and body.

To tune into the older, quieter, instinctive brain requires that you learn techniques to override your noisy, demanding younger brain (sometimes called the "monkey mind" because it's always grabbing at something new). This is the reason that spiritual leaders and philosophers, from Buddha to Jesus, Marcus Aurelius, Talmud scholars, the early Catholics, and Eckhart Tolle, encourage people to meditate, pray, and practice stillness. Acting from a place of calm is the best way to practice nunchi.

Stillness is simple, but it is not easy. Some people recoil at the thought of meditation and prayer, and I cannot convince them otherwise. But there are some "secular" methods you can use to still your mind if these options don't appeal.

You can do what I sometimes do when I feel my brain whirring hotly: in my mind, I will repeat or summarize every sentence the person says, as they are speaking. The exercise keeps me from being fidgety; it prevents me from interrupting; and it makes me look as if I am listening rapturously—because I actually am! Listening to someone is the fastest way to earn someone's trust and affection. This is because (as many great minds have noted before me), after food and shelter, the greatest human need is feeling that you are heard. Most people don't even really care whether you agree with them, only that you are listening.

Nunchi blocker 3:
Extroversion is valued over introversion

Extroverts are for some reason considered healthy and happy, while introverts are considered to be antisocial and dark. When one person in a long-term couple is an extrovert and the other is an introvert, they can often get into the same fight over and over at social gatherings: "Why are you off in the corner when our friends are here?" In most cases, the couple's friends will side with the extrovert and drag the quiet one to the center of attention to "pull their weight" socially.

The extroverts in this situation should examine their assumptions: why are you sure the introvert is not contributing to the room's atmosphere? If the introvert's distance makes you uncomfortable, why do you assume it's their fault and not yours? Can't you just pretend you're all in a nineteenth-century drawing room and everyone is there because it's the warmest room in the house, and you're all free to embroider, sleep, play whist, or whatever you want?

If you get a chance, try to have a chat with that introvert and get to know them. Likely you'll find that they know more about the dynamics of your social group than anyone. Their pulling away from the room allows them to pick up the overall room dynamics and nonverbal cues that extroverts may miss.

Nunchi blocker 4:
Jagged edges are valued over roundness

One of my favorite books growing up was Roald Dahl's beloved children's novel *James and the Giant Peach*. James, an orphan, is given magic crocodile tongues and accidentally spills them on the ground, resulting in a mutant gargantuan peach, in which he travels the world with a ragtag team of enormous mutant insects. In one scene, the peach gets attacked by sharks off the coast of Portugal, but never fear, the peach is too big and round for the sharks to get their mouths around, and all is well.

This story has always made me think of nunchi, and of the nunchi-ful aim of being like James's giant peach: round, expansive, with no jagged edges for anyone to grab hold of and use against you. Be a peach, be impervious to sharks.

Western society tends to reward pushy behavior. It makes sense: sharp-elbowed people are trying to get your attention, so of course we notice them more. But sharp elbows create jagged edges, which leads to two results: first, those edges may cut people, whether you wanted to or not; and second, you're giving other people an edge—a handle—to grab hold of, and they may not let go. Stay round, and your interactions with others will be smooth and easy.

You don't have to alter your behavior radically. Roundness is more a matter of *being* than doing.

How can you "be round"? The next time you find yourself in a conflict, don't just say whatever comes to mind. First, take a deep breath and ask yourself two simple questions before you think or act: "What am I doing and why?"

Sounds stupid, right? But it works. It doesn't even matter what the answer to that question is. By asking yourself what you're doing, you're getting out of your own mind and plugging into your outside environment—you're creating roundness.

The question creates an *immediate* stabilizing force in your brain, as if a rocking boat were suddenly to become still.

Are you about to chastise a colleague for bad work? Ask yourself, "What am I doing and why?" This does not mean you can't chastise your incompetent colleague—go right ahead; they probably deserve it. But that interaction is much more likely to go in your favor if you ask yourself that question first.

Even if you don't tone down your behavior or your words, you are going to handle that situation with much more control. If you don't, you're behaving from a place of instability and confusion. Try drawing a circle while sitting on a rocking boat—you can't. You'll just end up creating jagged edges.

Nunchi blocker 5:
Individualism is valued over collectivism

In Korea, if a child is impatient—for example, if they are waiting in a long line at the buffet table and complain, "We've been waiting forever! I'm hungry!"—the parent will not say, "Oh, you poor thing! I have grapes in my purse and they're already sliced in halves." They will say, "Are you the only person in the world?" (*Seh-sang eh nuh man isso.*) It's a very common parental chastisement. In other words, "Yeah, kid, everyone in this line is hungry, which you'd realize if you had any nunchi." Or to put it another way: "It's not all about you!" It's a hugely important part of a Korean up-bringing, and a crucial concept in nunchi.

Koreans teach this concept to their children in all sorts of ways. For example, Korean schools don't usually have cleaners. The students form groups and take turns cleaning the classroom each day after school. It's meant to provide several life lessons. For one, the tidier you are, the less time it takes to clean up. For another, it instills an awareness of the class as a single hive: what's good for one is good for all.

In 2017, there was a viral video of a car accident that had taken place in South Korea, in a long tunnel. Within one minute, all the cars in the tunnel created a "path of life" so the ambulance could enter the tunnel as soon as it arrived. Each driver rapidly pulled their car over to their far right and parked it up against the tunnel walls to clear space in the middle of the road. There are similar videos from China and Germany. It's pretty amazing to watch, and it can only happen in a culture that values collectivism and not just individualism.

In some cultures—those that place individualism at a premium—the "path of life" would not be possible. A significant proportion of the drivers would not have enough nunchi to understand what the other drivers were doing. Or they'd have noticed other cars were peeling off to the side and said, "What are all these idiots doing? Oh, cool, now there's a clear path for me to drive through this tunnel! Whoo!" And then they'd have been responsible for blocking the ambulance that was trying to get to the accident. Congratulations, murderers.

For many of us, the word "collectivism" just sounds dirty. Some of you probably winced at the sight of the word, or thought of old Soviet propaganda videos. But don't worry: you don't have to give up your individualism; you just have to acknowledge that you are part of a hive mind.

The next time you're at a sporting event or watching one on television, take note of the instances when the spectators all seem to be thinking the same thing: at U.S. baseball games or FIFA World Cup soccer matches, for example, people will do the "wave" (aka "Mexican wave"), where sections of the crowd stand and sit quickly, one column of seats after the other, to create the image of a ripple going across the stadium; and at rugby games in Britain, fans might start singing "Swing Low, Sweet Chariot." Who tells the fans when it's the right time in the game to start doing this? How did it spread globally? No one really knows. These examples show that we are already in a collective. By extension, this means our behavior affects others whether we like it or not.

The goal here is not to undo your biases—you really can't; they're part of your hardwiring. But being aware of them will set you on the right path toward nunchi. "Awareness" isn't just some annoying modern catchword; it's a way of telling your brain that you're ready to take a giant leap toward living your very best life.

QUICK QUIZ

Fooled you. There will be no quiz for this chapter: overcoming biases is about opening the mind by asking yourself questions, not fixating on the right answers! Put differently: the question is the answer.

CHAPTER 4

No Nunchi, or How to Lose Friends and Alienate People*

LLOYD (PLAYED BY COMEDIAN JIM CARREY): What are the chances of a guy like you and a girl like me . . . ending up together?

MARY: Not good.

LLOYD: Not good like one in a hundred?

MARY: I'd say more like one in a million.

LLOYD: So you're telling me there's a chance?

Dumb and Dumber[A]

Any Korean will tell you that nunchi is more notable in its absence than its presence.

Those who lack nunchi make people's eyes roll or make them glance in consternation at each other; frequently,

---

* With apologies to Toby Young.

those without nunchi get kicked under the table for failing to see what is obvious to everyone else.

Take the following as a case in point. At a friendly restaurant dinner, everyone around the table was drinking wine, except for Eileen, who instead ordered one sparkling water after another. Also in attendance was Hazel, who was notoriously lacking in nunchi. Hazel kept pushing Eileen to drink wine, despite Eileen's repeated insistence that she was fine with water.

Even when others stepped in, Hazel wouldn't let it rest.

Later, when Hazel was told that Eileen was a recovering alcoholic, Hazel exclaimed, "How was I supposed to know? Eileen should have told me!" Hazel couldn't see that it wasn't Eileen's responsibility to explain her personal history to someone she didn't know very well. It was Hazel's responsibility to read the room and act appropriately.

Before speaking, Hazel should have thought to ask herself the following:

1. **(Basic nunchi)** Look closely at Eileen's face and expressions. Does she appear uncomfortable with your remarks? WHY WOULD I LOOK CLOSELY AT HER FACE, WHO DOES THAT? ➔ Game over.
2. **(Intermediate nunchi)** Does Eileen's husband seem surprised that Eileen is not drinking? NO ➔ The

husband probably knows Eileen best, and he is not worried, so why should I be?

3. **(Ninja-level nunchi)** Is Eileen slowly sipping one sparkling water, or is she ordering one after the other? → THE LATTER. This may be the compulsion of someone who used to have a drinking problem.

Have you ever noticed that when someone says angrily, "I'm not a mind reader! It's not my fault!" about 90 percent of the time it really *is* their fault?

Such protests are the hallmark of someone with no nunchi. The social, professional, and happiness cost of such an attitude can be very high. If you have no nunchi, *people will irrationally hate you* without knowing why (I'm not exaggerating at all). At the very least, they may just not want you around.

People react to the nunchi-challenged in the same way that they might react to a person with horrible breath: they might feel petty about it, they might not even know why they find them repellent, all they know is that they don't like being around that person and can't wait for them to leave.

But how can you tell if *you* have bad nunchi?

If your nunchi is really bad, then you probably can't even tell. It's an extension of what psychologists call the

Dunning-Kruger effect, which is the cognitive bias that prevents a really stupid person from knowing that they are stupid. The good news is that if you are self-reflective enough to read this book, you have already demonstrated a desire to get your head out of your ass; thus, you are very capable of improving your nunchi.

If you have friends or loved ones who care enough to tell you that you have bad nunchi, consider yourself lucky. Realistically, though, there's a good chance that no one will tell you outright. If forced to respond to a direct question such as "What did I do to annoy everyone?," they might say, "I can't really put my finger on it."

In Korea, you might say that you don't like a person because they give you a bad *kibun*, which is the Korean word for mood as a sort of full-body experience. Tell a Korean friend you don't want to go on a date with Mr. Dreamboat from school because he gives you a bad *kibun*, and your friend will nod and not press the matter. It is understood and accepted that you would trust your nunchi about such a thing, but bad luck for Mr. Dreamboat, who may be unaware that his poor nunchi is putting off the ladies.

If you have poor nunchi, all is not lost. The first step to fixing a problem, the saying goes, is recognizing you have a problem. Here are some self-diagnostic questions to see whether you are a no-nunchi:

A NUNCHI SELF-ASSESSMENT QUIZ

Which of the following scenarios have you experienced?

A. You have been told any of the following: "Read the room"; "Yes, thanks, we heard you the first time"; or "What do you want, a medal?"

B. You're in a conference room at work, waiting for a meeting to start. To break the silence, you say, "Is this another one of George's idiotic meetings that could have been covered in an email?," only for George to wave at you from the corner of the room.

C. You hassle a colleague for being late on Thursday morning, only to be pulled aside and told, "You know he's been taking his mother for chemo every Thursday morning since September, right?"

D. You are broaching what you think is an important topic. Someone responds by muttering, "Bad timing."

E. Your friends will see you one-on-one but have suddenly stopped inviting you to group outings.

F. People repeatedly glance at each other while you are talking.

G. After speaking, you are met by a long, inexplicable silence from everyone in the room.

If three or more of these scenarios seem familiar to you, you would benefit from working on your nunchi.

If you look and listen, the answers are all right in front of you. You don't have to go through life feeling like a victim and wondering why bad things always seem to blindside you. Nunchi makes life more navigable and within your control.

The Eight Deadly No-Nunchi Archetypes

If you've ever watched first-round auditions for *The X Factor* or any of those other talent shows, you absolutely know what it looks like when someone has no nunchi. The show producers intentionally throw in people who aren't just bad singers—that would be boring—but who are completely convinced they're brilliant. In other words, people with no nunchi.

Every version of *The X Factor* or *[Country]'s Got Talent* in the entire world includes these nunchi-challenged auditions. Everyone loves them. Why? You might feel guilty making fun of someone just for being a bad singer. But you rarely feel guilty crucifying a bad singer who is entirely convinced he or she is great.

The singer with no nunchi has demonstrated tone-deafness in both the literal sense and the sense of ignoring social cues. Either their friends are afraid to tell them they have no talent, or they haven't got any friends (or they don't listen to them). It's human nature to believe that those who fail to take on board the reactions of those around them may have waived their right to sympathy from the audience.

You do not want to be like a bad *X Factor* contestant. It's simply not the case that ignorance is bliss, unless you think it would be blissful to have your friends peel away without explanation. You could also be missing out on opportunities to improve at singing (or another skill) or to choose a different passion where you could genuinely excel. One of the best things you can do for yourself if you want to improve your nunchi is to consider all criticism before either accepting or dismissing it.

What's more, when someone alerts you to nunchi-deficient behavior on your part, mortifying as it feels, thank them. They are doing you a huge favor and preventing you from embarrassing yourself. Do not blame them for not having told you "before," whatever nonsense you mean by "before." Think of it as like having spinach in your teeth—sure, it's embarrassing when someone tells you, but wouldn't you rather know before you go grinning obliviously at everyone you meet and scaring children? Take the feedback for what it is: an attempt to help you.

I believe that there are different subspecies of the nunchi-challenged. You might recognize yourself, your friends, frenemies, coworkers, or relatives among these eight deadly no-nunchi archetypes:

No-nunchi archetype 1:
The ones who cannot read the room

This is the most common variety of no-nunchi, and is usually the result of cluelessness rather than malice. This obliviousness frequently comes from being overly anxious and wrapped up in yourself rather than considering the room as a whole.

Consider someone like Catherine, an essentially good but self-centered person whose failure to read the room affected her relationships more than she knew. Her colleague Ben was changing the background photo on his computer desktop to one of himself and another man, when Catherine peered over his shoulder.

She joked, "Hey, Ben, you gonna change your desktop every time you get a new boyfriend? Is there even enough time in the day for that?"

Everyone's jaw dropped in horror. Ben's lip quivered, and he excused himself to step outside. One of Catherine's colleagues told her, "That guy in the photo? That's Ben's boyfriend, who died a few months ago of lupus-related kidney failure. Where have you been?"

When Ben returned to the office, Catherine apologized profusely and sincerely: "I had no idea, that's terrible, please forgive me." Later, Catherine bought Ben a pastry and apologized again, but it didn't make up for her crassness.

Could Catherine be faulted for not knowing about Ben's boyfriend's death? Maybe not. On the other hand, why was Catherine the only one on the team who didn't know? Ben had taken a leave of absence when the incident occurred, and Catherine apparently hadn't noticed. Also, if Catherine had been paying attention to everyone's faces while Ben was putting up the photo of his boyfriend, she'd have noticed the looks of sympathy. And why did she feel the need to comment on his desktop photo at all?

This wasn't just a single nunchi faux pas on Catherine's part; it snowballed because she hadn't been paying attention to her environment for some time. Obliviousness may not be the result of malice, but it can come across as malice to others, so be careful: pay attention.

No-nunchi archetype 2:
The stalkers who think they're romantics

Rom-coms of the Richard Curtis variety (*Love Actually* being the worst culprit) may or may not be responsible for a widespread misconception that wearing down someone's resistance by embarrassing them in public is a really good way to get a romantic partner. Both men and women are guilty of this. It's not romantic; it's a self-centered view of the world.

Take the case of Rainer, an opera singer, who had landed

his first lead role. His opening night was a triumph: the audience gave him a standing ovation and his father and his ninety-year-old grandmother, seated in the front row, had tears of pride streaming down their faces. For Rainer, it was an evening so perfect that nothing could have ruined it.

Nothing, that is, except for Ashleigh, the unstable ex-girlfriend he had not seen for ten years.

As Rainer was basking in his applause, Ashleigh leaped on to the stage and presented him with a large bouquet of flowers. Rainer was confused; he did not recognize her until she gave him a big hug and said, "Sweetie, I'm so proud of you." Then his look went from confusion to terror. The audience chuckled, assuming this was a spouse or girlfriend. Emboldened by what she interpreted as the audience's encouragement, Ashleigh remained onstage and followed Rainer into the wings as the curtain fell, demanding his attention, and failing to pick up on just how bizarre and uncomfortable he found the situation.

In the end Rainer was forced to be very rude to Ashleigh to get her to leave him alone.

Rainer's debut for his first-ever role should have been a night to cherish, but he doesn't remember it fondly, and it's because of Ashleigh. Don't be like Ashleigh: only bad things can happen if you think you are the star of a movie and everyone else is a side character whose feelings don't matter except insofar as they further your own agenda, romantic or otherwise.

No-nunchi archetype 3:
The ones who cannot read between the lines

Many of us have friends who have to have things spelled out for them, and sometimes even then they still don't get it. Of course, communication is a two-way street, and often misunderstandings are no one person's fault. Nonetheless, certain people seem to misunderstand things far more than average. At times it leads to awkwardness for all parties concerned.

Alice frequently complained that her new boyfriend, Stan, could never take a hint. One night, Alice said, "I think it's better you go back home tonight to sleep; I have to get up really early tomorrow." Stan said, "Oh, don't worry, I don't mind if you get up early! In fact, I could probably stand to try this 'early to bed, early to rise' thing." Alice tried to drop stronger hints until finally she had to say, "Stan, please, you've been here all week and I really want the bed to myself just this one night." Stan was upset and said, "Fine, why didn't you say so?" As if Alice hadn't been attempting to do that very thing all along.

If someone repeatedly states something that seems bafflingly oblique to you, such as "Wow, would you look at the time" or "Well, I've got a really busy day tomorrow," it is a sign that you may need to think a little harder about what might be behind their words.

Finding other people's verbal communication oblique or confusing is often a signal that we need to pay more attention to their nonverbal cues.

No-nunchi archetype 4:
The ones who "show off their Chinese calligraphy to Confucius"

This archetype suffers from something akin to "mansplaining," although this behavior is gender-neutral. If you vaunt your knowledge about something in front of an actual expert on that topic, the Koreans say: "That's like trying to show off your Chinese calligraphy in front of Confucius." This archetype is so lacking in nunchi that they pontificate without bothering to find out whether they are speaking to the world specialist.

Take Nimrod, for example, who gave an unsolicited dinner party lecture to Nikola about how a computer's RAM makes it run faster. Nothing too weird about that, except that Nikola had a PhD in computer science from MIT and had worked on the IBM supercomputer project that defeated Garry Kasparov at chess.

Nikola was too polite to embarrass Nimrod by revealing her credentials, but the reactions of the others around the table should have been a clue that this situation was excruciating for everyone involved. If Nimrod had asked Nikola even a few questions about herself, if he had thought more about observing and less about speaking, he would have made a much better impression on everyone.

No-nunchi archetype 5:
The ones who think everyone is just playing hard to get

My favorite literary example of good and bad nunchi would be Lizzy Bennet and Mr. Collins from Jane Austen's *Pride and Prejudice*. Lizzy has wildly quick nunchi, picking up on body language and always able to grasp the absurdity of a situation (even if she cannot speak it aloud). Mr. Collins has no nunchi; he is a tool.

For those who don't know the story, Lizzy and Mr. Collins are distant cousins; the latter is heir to the home in which Lizzy grew up. As with many no-nunchi unfortunates, Mr. Collins is a well-meaning person, but that almost makes it worse: Lizzy hates herself for hating him, which makes her resent him even more. This leads to the most awkward proposal scene in all of English literature. In typical no-nunchi fashion, Collins has severely overestimated his attractiveness as a partner. Despite Lizzy's clear signals and the fact that anyone else could see she is appalled at the proposal, Collins assumes she is playing hard to get, and tells her: "As I must therefore conclude that you are not serious in your rejection of me, I shall choose to attribute it to your wish of increasing my love by suspense, according to the usual practice of elegant females."

This is a spectacular failure of nunchi, as it manages to ignore both Lizzy's words and her physical discomfort. It is clear that anyone who is so impervious to the reactions of others must be thinking more of themselves than they are of the other person.

Don't be Mr. Collins. If you have any doubt at all about how your message—in love or in anything else—is being received, back off and try to read the room instead of pushing your own agenda.

No-nunchi archetype 6:
The ones who take all compliments too literally

Let's say you're a writer who is having trouble getting published, despite the encouragement of friends and family, who tell you they love your writing. Do you keep trying? On the one hand, you might be the next Stephen King, whose first novel, *Carrie*, was rejected by thirty publishers before Doubleday bought it. Maybe your next attempt will be successful, just like King was with his thirty-first publisher—the legendary "and the rest is history" moment.

On the other hand, it is also possible that your friends and family love your writing because they love *you*, and that means they aren't best placed to judge your talent.

How can you know whether you should keep going? What makes it even more confusing is that successful people often say in awards speeches, "Never give up." And your friends will echo that advice.

I, too, would encourage not giving up on your craft...but you should definitely give up on getting advice about it from friends and family, who are too close to you to be objective. One important component of nunchi—and, thus, of success—is to be unafraid of the truth, even if it's not what you want to hear. The late musician John Lennon went to art college as a teen, and looking now at his remaining drawings, it seems he was reasonably talented. But if he'd stubbornly insisted on being the next Van Gogh just because his mother put his pictures on her fridge, then he'd never have been a Beatle.

In writing, as in all other things, you must be able to distinguish between a compliment offered in admiration of your talent, and a compliment offered by someone who loves you and doesn't want to hurt your feelings. True nunchi means asking yourself, "Who is offering this compliment and why?," and listening to the answer, even if it's not what you want to hear.

No-nunchi archetype 7:
The bores

In French, the word *ennuyeux* can mean both "boring" and "annoying." If there's any language that reflects a profound understanding of human nature, it's French.

You'd think bores were harmless, and yet everyone hates them. As Oscar Wilde wrote, "A bore is someone who deprives you of solitude without providing you with company."

The bore isn't boring because their anecdotes lack car chases and explosions; they're boring because they don't listen, and so their responses don't match up with what the other person just said. So if someone says, "I'm sorry Gene's not here. I don't know if you heard that he was in a horrible car accident," the bore will say, "Well, one time I saw an accident too. There was this deer..." and go into irrelevant detail without even asking whether Gene is OK.

No one is ever a bore on purpose; usually it happens because someone is terrified of being silent. This is why the capacity for stillness and quiet is terribly important for good nunchi.

No one is more engaging than someone who listens to you, thus connecting to you. And no one is more boring than someone who changes topics to focus on themselves, or engages in one-upmanship with stories. People who do this aren't really listening to you in the first place; they're just waiting for their turn to talk.

Next time someone tells an anecdote or expresses their thoughts and feelings, try to pause for a few seconds and give a response that is not a personal story. It's *so* hard, right? It's very telling that we can barely think of anything to say that isn't a personal anecdote. But people don't need your story to be better than their story; they just need to know you're listening. You'll both get along better by the end of it.

No-nunchi archetype 8:
The ones who say, "But this is how we do it where I'm from"

Whether you mean "But this is how we do it..." in your old office, your hometown, or your culture, I. Don't. Care. Having quick nunchi means you adapt to your *current* situation, regardless of what you might have done or said in the past.

One unfortunate example of this, which attracted international media coverage, took place in New York City in 1997. A Danish tourist was dining in a restaurant in Manhattan's East Village (at the time, not New York's safest neighborhood) and left her fourteen-month-old baby outside on the sidewalk, in a stroller. Concerned passersby contacted the police. The child's parents were arrested on child endangerment charges. The baby was removed from their custody and placed in foster care for several days. The mother and the Danish press protested that in her native Denmark it was completely normal to leave babies outside in the fresh air rather than dragging them into a smoke-filled restaurant.

While I don't approve of the child being removed from its parents, I do think the tourist was in the wrong here. What you do in your native country should not override your nunchi. Had she looked around for even five seconds, she'd have noticed: 1) that the area was not nearly as safe as most parts of Denmark; and 2) that no one else had left their babies outside.

This wasn't an instance of Americans being puritanical—the concerned New Yorkers were trying to prevent some marauder potentially kidnapping or hurting the child. At the time, Nicholas Scoppetta, the Commissioner of the Administration for Children's Services, told the *New York Times*, "To leave a child unattended for an hour on a city street in New York is pretty inappropriate...I don't think you should expect the Police Department to make inquiries about whether this is acceptable in Denmark."[5] This statement is a perfect illustration of the fact that no one, but no one, will forgive your lack of nunchi. No one cares about your good intentions. And sometimes the stakes are very high indeed.

In an unfamiliar environment, see what other people are doing and give them the benefit of the doubt: it's likely that they're doing it for a reason.

You've probably noticed a major thread running through these eight no-nunchi archetypes: they can't read the room.

As you no doubt have gleaned, anyone who thinks that a lack of nunchi will garner nothing more serious than the occasional eye roll from your friends is sadly mistaken. You're dead wrong if you think people's disapproval is their problem, or if you think that ignorance is bliss. A lack of awareness of social cues can mean losing friends, people's respect, your job, or even, like the Danish mother, your child (don't worry, she got the baby back!).

You are a tourist in a former Iron Curtain country. You are awakened one morning by a loud siren. You stick your head out of the window and hear an announcement from giant loudspeakers, left over from the martial-law era. You notice people on the street are scurrying. Do you:

A. Say to yourself, "Oh, those alarms are so annoying. I guess you can take the nation out of communism, but you can't take communism out of the nation."

B. Scream at everyone on the street to chill the hell out because you're trying to sleep.

C. Go back to bed.

D. Start packing your bags.

Correct answer: D. This one's obvious in theory, but this exact situation happened to me and my sister in Prague in 2002. Our first reaction to the panic was to take it seriously and insist on getting to the airport to take an earlier flight out of the country. Just before leaving, I warned some hungover tourists in our hotel that they'd better evacuate, and they gently mocked me. Once at the airport, though, we found out that Prague was experiencing the worst flood it had had since 1890—it subsequently became known as the Hundred Years Flood. The whole city was submerged. We boarded one of the last flights out of Prague. Had we listened to those tourists and chilled out, we would have been stuck in a strange city for days during a natural disaster.

Did we speak Czech? No. However, we have previously lived in countries with loudspeakers on the streets, and if someone uses them to make a citywide announcement, there is always a reason, and it's not to announce that there's a massive bread sale at the local bakery. It is always an emergency.

CHAPTER 5

Two Eyes, Two Ears, One Mouth

We are given two ears and one mouth that
we may listen twice as much as we speak.[6]

Epictetus (c. AD 55–135), Enchiridion

As soon as Korean children can communicate, their parents teach them the importance of "stilling": listening and paying attention to what other people are doing. Being a three-year-old is no excuse for having no nunchi; in fact, Koreans have a saying: "A habit acquired at age three remains till age eighty." For example, if everyone is standing on the right-hand side of the escalator and leaving the left side empty, the child has to realize that maybe there is a reason for this, namely that standing on the right creates a path on the left for people to walk on if they're in a hurry. So, don't be the sole rude child who obliviously stands on the left. The child should be able to work this out without their parents having to spell it out for them, as this kind of self-reliance is part of the whole nunchi education.

In Korea, the Western "kids will be kids" attitude does not fly. Children are made to take responsibility for themselves at a very early age.

At Korean school, students are expected to infer everything for themselves. Teachers won't give students convenient written lists of supplies to bring for the next day's complicated art project. They'll just say, "We're making lampshades," and the students have to work out on their own what materials to bring for that. If you don't bring the right wire cutters, that's too bad; the school doesn't keep tools around and, even if they did, they would never lend them to you, because you're the one who messed up.

Sometimes teachers will be intentionally vague about vital information, such as where exams are taking place. And yet, guess what? Mysteriously, everyone manages to bring the right wire cutters and show up in the right exam room (even non-Korean-speaking me), because they are taught from an early age to work things out for themselves. You get your information by asking the right people at the right time and, more importantly, by keeping your eyes and ears open to take note of what everyone else is doing. That's the early nunchi education.

A Western parent might recoil at this: "I don't want to raise a lemming! I'm trying to teach my kid that just because everyone else is jumping off a bridge, that doesn't mean they should do it too." Yet instinctively, you know that there is wisdom in crowds. For example, all New Yorkers are familiar with this unspoken rule: if a subway car is empty on an otherwise crowded train, there is always a reason. Often that reason involves urine. Don't enter. The crowd isn't always right, but on public transport it usually is.

You use nunchi every time you leave the house. On an unconscious level, you use it to decide whom to ask for directions—on the London Underground, you ask the person who's clearly commuting to work and has thus done this route a million times, not the tourist stressing over a map. You use your nunchi to determine whether the eccentric sitting next to you on the bus is just curious about the book you're reading, or whether they're going to flash their genitals.

Maybe you've been in a train car with your noise-canceling headphones on and your music all the way up. You don't hear the guard's announcement on the loudspeaker, telling everyone, "Due to a problem with the signaling system, this train is being delayed and also will only be making certain stops." But your nunchi tells you that your fellow passengers look very annoyed and have started speaking to each other. So you realize something unexpected has happened on the journey.

Driving a car requires nunchi as well. Instinctively, you sense which drivers will let you pass, and which are going to go absolutely mental if you attempt it.

When you go to the shops, you use your nunchi to work out which line for the cashier will go the fastest. You might initially take a spot behind someone whose shopping cart seems to be the least full, then switch to another line when you notice that they've got 100 Kinder Surprise chocolate eggs, each of which has to be individually scanned. Instinctively, you steer away from the line where the checkout person looks ready for a break, or where a customer is smoothing out fistfuls of coupons.

Wouldn't it be great if nunchi worked for you this easily and naturally in all areas of life? Happily, this is very achievable; all you have to do is train yourself to look and listen.

And if you don't? Well, the consequences can be dire, as evidenced by the abundant Korean children's books with titles like *The Child with No Nunchi* or *The Elephant with No Nunchi*. I'll save you the trouble of reading them and give you the upshot: the child and elephant have no friends.

You needn't have been raised on moralistic Korean children's books or in a brutal Korean school to learn nunchi. I've done all that for you and have distilled it into these eight rules.

The Eight Rules of Nunchi

1. First, empty your mind. Lose your preconceptions in order to observe with discernment.
2. Be aware of the Nunchi Observer Effect. When you enter a room, you change the room. Understand your influence.
3. If you just arrived in the room, remember that everyone else has been there longer than you. Watch them to gain information.
4. Never pass up a good opportunity to shut up. If you wait long enough, most of your questions will be answered without you having to say a word.
5. Manners exist for a reason.
6. Read between the lines. People don't always say what they are thinking and that's their prerogative.
7. If you cause harm unintentionally, it's sometimes as bad as if you'd caused it intentionally.
8. Be nimble, be quick.

Rule #1: First, empty your mind

There is a Bruce Lee quote that frequently does the rounds on social media as an inspirational meme, and with good reason. Lee said, "Empty your cup, so that it may be filled." When it comes to reading the room, think of the room as a pool of water, and yourself as the cup. How will you be able to discern the temperature and the taste of the water if your own cup is already full to the brim?

When your mind is full of assumptions about people and situations, it is hard to see what is right in front of you, and to behave in the most appropriate manner.

Amanda worked for a multinational company in London, and was invited to a drinks reception for Dan, the visiting head of the New York office. Amanda had never visited America, but felt she knew a lot about Americans from watching movies and television. In her opinion, Americans were loud, brash, and very informal in their interactions with others.

When she found herself in a group conversation with Dan, Amanda was overly concerned with making a good impression on "the American," and didn't pay attention to the cues in the room itself. Dan's manner was not informal at all; in fact most of the people around him treated him with deference. So when Dan finished an anecdote with one hand raised in the air, it was only Amanda who overthought the situation based on her preconceptions, and stepped forward to give him the friendly high five she assumed he was inviting. His limp palm and horrified expression soon corrected her.

Poor Amanda thought she was doing the right thing: no one wants to be left hanging when they've invited a high five. But she was basing her behavior on the beliefs she had brought into the room, not on the interactions that were visible in the room. If her focus had been on reading everyone else, she would have saved herself a lot of embarrassment.

Emptying your mind can mean anything from taking two minutes to close your eyes and focus on your breath before you enter a space, to just mentally reminding yourself to "stay in the room" when you feel your thoughts beginning to spiral.

Before entering any social situation, check to see how you feel. There's a mnemonic for this that anxiety sufferers use: HALT, which stands for hungry, angry, lonely, and tired. Are you any of those things? If so, ask yourself, "How might that affect the way I go into this room and what I see there?" Remember the saying: "we don't see people as they are; we see people as *we* are."

In the long term, practices such as meditation can help you to respond to situations with discernment, instead of reacting in a panicked manner.

Empty your mind, instead of spilling your overfull cup on others.

Rule #2: Be aware of the Nunchi Observer Effect

There is a concept in quantum physics called the Observer Effect, which states that you change things just by the act of observing them. It's the same when a person enters a room: you change the atmosphere just by being there, so there's no need to make a big song and dance as you arrive.

A nunchi expert will tell you that instead of trying to make a splash when you enter a room, you should first honor the room, which will help remind you of Nunchi Rule #1: Empty your mind.

Of the everyday Jewish traditions, one of my favorites is the kissing of the mezuzah upon entering the threshold of a home and some of the rooms in it. The mezuzah, a tiny rolled-up scroll housed in a small tube or box, is affixed to the right side of a door frame at approximately shoulder height. The scroll is inscribed with the Shema prayer, which begins, "Hear, O Israel" (note the word "hear"; it's practically a nunchi reminder!) and includes two sections of the Torah: Deuteronomy 6:4–9 and 11:13–21. Kissing the mezuzah is a way of honoring God, but I also like to think of it as a way of honoring the room, of saying hi to it. One does it even if the room or home is otherwise empty.

The mezuzah is an amazing tactile reminder of the importance of inner stillness. Many religions have physical objects that remind people to think outside themselves. Prayer beads come to mind: Catholics, Muslims, and Buddhists all have their own version of prayer beads. Humans are deeply affected by their sense of touch, and talismans arose out of that need. In fact, these types of physical objects are an embodiment of nunchi: using all of your senses as a way of engaging with the world.

Regardless of your faith, or even if you are an atheist, I highly, emphatically recommend that you think of a room as if there were a mezuzah on the door frame—entering mindfully and deliberately, and thinking about something other than yourself. It doesn't have to be God, it just has to be Not All About You.

Years ago, I had a lovely work colleague whom I'll call Viola, who invited me to a small dinner party at her home one Friday. There was a snowstorm that day that caused horrid traffic, and I arrived late. As soon as I entered the apartment, I said breathlessly to a bunch of people I had never met, "OH SHIT I'M SO SORRY I'M LATE THIS WEATHER IS SO SHIT."

Everyone looked uncomfortable.

Out of nervousness, I rattled on, "I WOULD'VE BEEN HERE EARLIER EXCEPT I STOPPED BY THE STORE TO PICK UP THIS BOTTLE AND THE LINE WAS GOING ALL THE WAY ROUND THE BLOCK THEN I RAN ALL THE

WAY HERE SO I'M OUT OF BREATH WOW I SOUND ASTHMATIC I HOPE EVERYONE LIKES SANCERRE?"

They sat in silence. I kept trying to win people over with more babble. They were exceedingly polite, but I knew something was wrong.

The following Monday at work, Viola cleared up the mystery of everyone's discomfort. On the Friday evening, just before I burst in, one of the other guests was making a big announcement to the group: she had inoperable pancreatic cancer, was not doing chemo, and had weeks or months to live. Apparently, the last thing she had said before I started yelling was, "I'm just going to focus on quality of life and creating memories for my husband."

I guess I became one of those memories.

Obviously, there was no way I could have known that. And Viola did not tell me this story in a reproachful way. I apologized, flustered, for barreling in with my interminable apology, and she said, "No, of course! There's no way you could have known. Think nothing of it. I just wanted to let you know."

But I could tell that I would never be invited back to Viola's house.

Now you might be thinking, "Hey, Euny, that's a very awkward coincidence, but you did nothing wrong. If they don't see that, they're being unfair."

True, I hadn't done anything "wrong," but intent is not impact. They associated me with ill feeling, and they probably felt guilty about having those ill feelings, but it's hard to get that stench off the whole situation.

HOW I SHOULD HAVE USED MY NUNCHI

Despite my lateness to the party, there was *no reason* why I couldn't have honored the room before crossing the threshold. It's not as if I were delivering live bodily organs for transplant; I could have taken a few seconds to do my "nunchi room-entry" ritual, i.e. quietly assessing the existing climate of the room rather than immediately changing it like some obstreperous pizza-delivery guy. Later at home, as I sifted through my mental screenshots of the room, I remembered the following details:

- When Viola's husband answered the door, he whispered "welcome" very quietly, which should have been my cue that either something was off, or I should *at least* have turned on my nunchi switch to see what might be happening.
- When I entered the room, no one was smiling—odd for a dinner party. I assumed they were annoyed at my lateness, because when you don't use your nunchi, you think everything is about you.

- The terminally ill woman was not eating or drinking anything.
- The man next to the terminally ill woman had her
  hand in his, clasping it in both his hands.

This is very typical of nunchi-lacking errors. I was so
preoccupied with my own situation that I was sure it was
going to be number one in everyone's minds. I wanted to
reassure them I wasn't inconsiderate. In fact, I achieved the
opposite.

Rule #3: If you just arrived in the room, remember that everyone else has been there longer than you

When you're flying a kite, you can't just throw it up to the
sky and expect it to soar like a graceful hawk. The first
thing you do is gauge which way the wind is blowing, usually by wetting your index finger and holding it up in the
air or observing the trees or grass blowing around you.
Nunchi works on exactly the same principle. And remember that if anything is certain about wind, it's that it
changes when it wants to, not when *you* want it to.

Having quick nunchi means being able to eye-assess what
is happening in the room as you arrive, and continuing to
recalibrate your assessment continuously, as things change.

Social situations can be incredibly fluid—even at a funeral there are moments of humor, and people can be very grateful for them—so be aware and be adaptable to what is actually happening, rather than to what you think should be happening. For example, at some Irish wakes, people tell funny stories about the deceased. But that doesn't mean it's open season at any Irish funeral to joke about how the old lady, God bless her soul, bonked half the village before she turned seventeen. You should aim to make your presence in the room rounded and smooth, like James's giant peach.

I once heard a story about the Queen that shows her to be a master of quick nunchi, even if she has never heard the word. At a Buckingham Palace banquet, a visiting foreign dignitary picked up the finger bowl full of water, intended for washing his hands, and drank from it. The guests around him gasped at his social faux pas, but to save him from embarrassment the Queen simply picked up her own finger bowl and drank from hers too. Led by her example, others followed suit.

The Queen demonstrated exceptional nunchi: she could have politely indicated to her guest that the water was not intended for drinking, but instead she saw a situation that could cause him embarrassment, and took swift action to defuse it. Those who also drank their finger bowls showed swift nunchi: they overcame their ingrained knowledge that drinking from the finger bowl wasn't socially acceptable, and saw that in this situation it was now necessary.

Stay aware of when the wind might change, and be sure you change with it in order to maintain harmony in the room as a whole.

No one is suggesting that you should feel pressured into doing something that you know to be wrong, just because everyone else is doing it. It is not nunchi-ful to join in with bullying or harassment or other antisocial behaviors, if that is what is happening in the room.

Rule #4: Never pass up a good opportunity to shut up

> *Il faut tourner sept fois sa langue dans sa bouche avant de parler.*
> *(You should turn your tongue in your mouth seven times before you speak.)*
>
> *A French proverb*
>
> *Words have legs.*
>
> *My mom*

When I was attending Korean school, no one ever raised their hands during class to ask a question. There was no rule against it; it simply wasn't done. Asking a question would be viewed as a selfish interruption: why cut the lecture short and rob everyone of an education just so you can clear up something for yourself?

This is shocking to most Westerners; often people think I'm exaggerating. But look at it this way: there were sixty students per class in those days, so if even just 10 percent of the class were to pose questions, no teaching would get done. Sure, your question might have been something others were wondering about too, but most likely the students would have learned more if you'd just let the teacher finish.

And if you still had a burning question after the lecture? No problem: you just had to see the teacher between classes or after school. They actively encouraged it and were very generous with their time.

This "no questions during class" custom is one of the reasons Korean children develop tremendous nunchi so quickly.

It was a point of huge culture shock for me, a twelve-year-old American kid. But I learned two lessons worth more than rubies: 1) if you wait long enough, most questions will be answered for you; 2) you learn more from listening than from speaking.

Think about your office meetings: many people ask questions to show off or brownnose the boss, or just to be seen to be participating. Are the people asking the most questions in meetings automatically getting respect or bo-nuses? Well, that depends. Sometimes asking a lot of questions shows you're engaged, but at other times those same questions will earn you side-eyes from your colleagues, who are fixated on the fact that it's 12:30 and the line at the taco place down the road is getting longer by the second. Read the room and don't always feel you have to ask every question that's in your head, especially just before lunch.

In twenty-first-century society, particularly in the West and especially in the Anglo world, loudness is valorized. Being quiet is associated with beta behavior. I find this hilarious and contradictory, since we also celebrate the stereotype of the "strong, silent type," like cowboys or steely military leaders.

Anyone skilled at negotiation will tell you that being silent puts you in a highly advantageous position. The only reason we don't hear more about silence is that quiet people by definition do not go on about how great it is to be quiet. They are unlikely to say, "I can see my silence is making you give more information, which is my whole objective." Nunchi is the better part of valor. Negotiation is the introvert's chance to show who's boss.

Imagine you have fallen in love with a house and are desperate to buy it. Obviously, you want the lowest price, while the seller and agent will want the highest price.

The agent asks whether you have kids. If you're a nunchi ninja, you may have already inferred that the agent is planning to tell you that the house is expensive because it's in a great area for schools. Or maybe you don't know where the question is going, but even your low-level nunchi reminds you to say as little as possible. Pause for five seconds—even though this will seem like an eternity—and say simply, "Why do you ask?"

Even if the agent has no agenda and is just being nosy, your verbal minimalism is still strategically a good idea. If you have made them nervous, that sets the tone that you are in a position of strength for the rest of the negotiation.

Let's say that your initial instinct was right, and the agent says, "The reason I ask is that the schools here are excellent, which is why you're paying a premium." Maybe the schools really are important to you; this doesn't mean you have to help the agent get a higher commission. All you need to say is, "I see."

At this point the agent is starting to worry. Your extreme economy of words is making them realize they're not going to charm you, and the only thing that might work is if they lower the price.

Obviously, this tactic might not work for this particular house. The owner may be inflexible about the price and that's not your fault. But it's still a victory, because the agent now knows—consciously or not—that you are not easily impressed. If you establish an image of stoicism from the very beginning, you'll be in a much stronger position for all the houses the agent shows you after that. At the very worst, you have nothing to lose.

Be the strong and silent type. The loudest person in a negotiation is not always the winner. Leave silence and space to allow people to come to you.

Rule #5: Manners exist for a reason

Those who dismiss nunchi are the same people who think that table manners are hoity-toity traps invented by the upper class to embarrass the lower class. This is false, false, false. If you really think that, please don't ever come to my house.

Manners serve a couple of useful purposes:

1. The very artifice of manners makes the room a safe space, just like rules in sports. It might be annoying to have to wait for everyone to be seated, or eat your soup without splashing it, but in doing so, you remind yourself to consider the comfort of others. This brings a feeling of instant calm and stability to the room and everyone in it.

2. Manners create a playing field for the guests. That field might not be a level one, but it is an invitation to coexist in this space and create healthy boundaries.

Table manners differ from culture to culture, and no one expects you to know all of them. But what people *will* expect you to do is to use your nunchi—whether they have heard of that word or not.

Let's use the example of bread plates. Sarah brought her new boyfriend, Magnus, to a dinner with old friends. He started to put bread on the small plate to his right. His girlfriend, seated to his left, whispered, "Darling, your bread plate is the one on the left. That's not yours." But Magnus, lacking good nunchi, was too embarrassed to listen to her and doubled down on his error, making a point of piling more bread on to the plate and plastering it with great slabs of butter.

Just one problem: when you take the wrong bread plate, it means someone else hasn't got one. The woman to his right looked up awkwardly and said to him, "I'm sorry, but I wonder whether you might be using my bread plate?" Magnus spent the rest of the evening muttering about how Sarah's friends were being snotty to him.

Yes, it was an honest mistake, but it was a failure of eye-measuring on his part not to watch what others were doing and follow accordingly. Magnus's error was unlike that of the foreign dignitary who drank from the finger bowl, because while the dignitary only (potentially) created awkwardness for himself, Magnus's failure to read the room created awkwardness for someone else.

An important caveat when it comes to manners and nunchi is to remember that manners exist to make everyone feel comfortable, rather than to make yourself feel superior because you know best. Loudly telling people what they should or shouldn't be doing at the dinner table is not good nunchi.

Rule #6: Read between the lines

A friend once told me, "If you want to know what someone is really saying, turn down the volume." This seems like a contradiction, but it's not. It means: don't take a person's words as being an exact reflection of their thoughts. Study the context, study nonverbal cues. In other words, don't judge a book by its cover. Often people's words are just that—a cover.

You might think that everyone owes it to you to say exactly what they're thinking, but they don't. Koreans would consider this an entitled attitude on your part. Sometimes you *do* have to be a mind reader and, with good nunchi, it's not as hard as you might imagine.

You've volunteered to be a host family to refugees from a war-torn country. At first, it's a delight: they're polite and quiet, they're tidy and considerate, they wash every dish they use, and, even though you don't speak their language, you can tell that after around 8 p.m. the parents chastise their kids if they make too much noise. When you're reading or at your computer, the family makes sure not to disturb you.

One day the mother asks, "Do many people in this country eat pork, like you?" You reply, "I guess if they like it, then yes." You think it's a weird question and yet you don't follow it up, even though your nunchi should have told you to inquire further.

Later, the father repeats the question: "Do people in this country eat pork every day?" Again, instead of asking what he means by that, you just brush it off. Only a month later do you discover that they are Muslim and aren't supposed to eat pork for religious reasons; they've been eating it this whole time because that's what you served, and they didn't want to be rude to their host.

You might be horrified or think, "It's ridiculous they didn't tell me! Asking whether the locals here eat pork is so passive-aggressive! What am I, a mind reader?"

But if you had good nunchi, you would have realized that there were literally dozens of clues that the family's culture had a very indirect, nonconfrontational style. Their careful consideration of your comfort should have signaled to you that they are used to people doing things without having to be asked. Everything about their behavior should have told you that they value making people feel at ease more than they value direct communication. So, yes, in that sense, you should have been a mind reader, or at least followed your instinct to explicitly ask them why they were so interested in how much pork people eat in this country.

Any time you find yourself thinking, "Jeez, I'm not a psychic," take it as a signal to yourself that your nunchi may be deficient in some way.

Rule #7: If you cause harm unintentionally, it's sometimes as bad as if you'd caused it intentionally

When you create ill feeling due to having no nunchi, you do not score points just because you did not *intend* to upset anyone. Nunchi is not like one of those contests where everyone gets a prize regardless of the actual outcome.

Karen was really into health and wellness, and liked to tell everyone about it. She felt amazing thanks to her new regime of intermittent fasting and weight training and, with the best possible intentions, she wanted everyone to feel as good as she did. Karen therefore offered positive reinforcement whenever she saw them taking steps toward a healthier lifestyle.

"Hey, have you lost a little weight, because you look *great*!"

"Have you been eating leafy greens, because I don't remember your skin glowing like this before?"

"If you ever want a partner at the gym, I'd be so happy to help you improve your upper-body strength."

It took a while before Karen realized her friends had begun avoiding her. Her focus on her own health regime had made her blind to how critical her "positive reinforcement" felt to others. Where she thought she was giving encouragement, they were hearing judgment of their habits.

Pro tip: asking others if they've lost weight is pretty much always terrible nunchi. They may have lost weight because of stress or illness or bereavement, and it's inappropriate to draw attention to it. If you must comment, a simple "You look great" is rarely taken as anything other than a compliment.

Just as ignorance of the law is no excuse to a judge, a lack of awareness is no excuse to the nunchi master. Without it you cannot be said to have good nunchi.

One benefit of improving your nunchi is that you will notice far fewer occasions where you accidentally offend a person.

Rule #8: Be nimble, be quick

As we've established, when someone is skilled in nunchi, Koreans don't say that person has "good nunchi," they say the person has "quick nunchi." The expression "slow and steady wins the race" does not apply to nunchi. Being right is sometimes useless if you're too slow.

When I think of the people with the quickest nunchi in film and fiction, the word "scrappy" comes to mind. A disproportionate number of nunchi ninjas are orphans: Tom Sawyer, Becky Sharp from Thackeray's *Vanity Fair*, the fairy-tale version of Dick Whittington, the protagonist from the film *Slumdog Millionaire* who wins the quiz show, and the little street urchin and spy Gavroche from *Les Misérables* (his parents are alive but might as well not be). Basically, there is a trope that hardship sharpens orphans' wits and, in turn, that their wits pull them out of hardship, which fits with what Koreans say about nunchi: it is the secret weapon of the disadvantaged.

For example, Tom Sawyer uses his nunchi to get out of the dreaded task of whitewashing his Aunt Polly's fence. He famously employs reverse psychology to convince his friends that he's having fun and they're missing out, thereby getting them to do the job for him. Though this might be an example of using nunchi for ill, this same quick thinking saves the lives of Tom and his friends throughout the novel. At the end of their adventures, Tom uses his quick nunchi to trick Huck Finn into staying on the straight and narrow path.

Gavroche uses his wits not just to beg for food on the streets of Paris, but to upgrade it from burned bread to white bread. His nunchi allows him on several occasions to see through disguises, which is why, at age eleven, he becomes the eyes and ears of an anti-monarchist revolutionary group. When bad-guy Inspector Javert tries to infiltrate the revolutionaries by posing as one of them, it's Gavroche's eagle eye that recognizes Javert is out of place, and he correctly concludes that he is a spy.

Putting Nunchi into Practice

Let's say you're at your favorite café with your best friend. The place is crowded and you're trying to work out where to perch yourself so as to maximize the likelihood that you get the next available table. You might both say things like, "Ooh, that guy looks like he's going to stand up—oh, never mind, he's just shifting his body weight to the other ass cheek." "Oh, that table, that one!... No, sorry, she was just getting up to get a sugar packet."

If you and your friend are in the habit of café-hopping together, you may have noticed that one of you is always right about which table will become free, and the other is far slower. The one who spots the soon-to-be-empty table first is the one with better nunchi.

A true nunchi ninja has an uncanny ability to predict human behavior.

Which of the following parties is most likely to leave the café first, thereby vacating a table for you to seize?

A. The starry-eyed couple gazing into each other's eyes

B. The solo hipster wearing noise-canceling headphones, with three empty coffee cups surrounding his laptop

C. Two uncomfortable-looking people in formal business attire

D. A group of young mothers with babies and a row of strollers by their side

If you guessed C, you're right, all things being equal. Most likely they're on a work break, aren't really friends in any true sense, and can't wait to get out of there. As for Answer A, the starry-eyed couple: you shouldn't perch there even if they appear to be close to finished. It's likely that they'll order dessert or another drink, so you have no real idea when they're going to leave. As for B, while it's true that people by themselves tend not to linger, all bets are off if they have their computer with them and are getting work done. And D: are you crazy? Do you have any idea how long it takes for a group of people to put children in strollers and wheel out of there one by one?

CHAPTER 6

Trusting Your First Impressions

When people show you who they are, believe them.

Maya Angelou

All the world's a stage,

And all the men and women merely players;

They have their exits and their entrances,

And one man in his time plays many parts.

William Shakespeare, As You Like It, Act II, Scene VII

As a young woman, Robyn was interviewed by a movie executive who promised he could do great things for her career. He was a well-known figure in the industry, and her friends and family all thought she was crazy when she turned the job down because she felt creeped out after her meeting with him. At the time she was unable to give any reason for this feeling, other than saying that he sat on top of his desk during part of the interview, which she saw as an indicator that he didn't mind crossing boundaries, trivial though they might be. For a long time, as she worked her way up the career ladder, Robyn questioned whether she had been right to decline the job, which would have opened many doors for her. Many years later, Mr. Creepy ended up being one of the high-profile men who lost their jobs after the #MeToo fallout.

Robyn had excellent nunchi. Even though she was desperate to get a job in the movie business, she didn't let that desire override her first impression that the executive was not to be trusted. She believed in her own instincts against the advice of her family and friends, and today she is confident that she made the right decision.

People tell you a lot about themselves when you first meet them, even if they don't say a word. Nunchi can help you to listen, but only if you remember Nunchi Rule #1: First, empty your mind. When you let go of your ideas about what you think should or should not be happening in a situation, you become open to understanding *what is actually happening.*

One of the most popular true-crime podcasts ever, *Dirty John*, tells the story of Debra Newell, a 59-year-old divorcée from California, who in 2014 met a dashing medical doctor named John Meehan. After only two months of dating, they married. Debra's oldest daughter, Jacquelyn, who was clearly a nunchi ninja, knew straight away that something was wrong with John. One big clue? John wore operating-room scrubs in public, everywhere he went. Jacquelyn wondered why was there never any blood or bodily fluids on his scrubs, if he had supposedly just come from surgery, and tried to warn her mother. Debra wouldn't listen to Jacquelyn.

As you've probably guessed, the Newells discovered that John was not a doctor; he was a nurse stripped of his license for stealing drugs from hospitals. They learned he was an opioid addict; that he had a criminal record a mile long; and that he had been homeless when he met Debra. She tried to divorce him, but that's when he started threatening her and her family. The only reason Debra was able to rid herself of John was that he died. He tried to stab Debra's younger daughter, Terra, who then killed John in self-defense.

This story features both someone with no nunchi (Debra, the mother) and two people with very quick nunchi (the two daughters). Debra's fear that she might have to spend her life alone convinced her that John was her "last chance" for love, and so strong was this fear that it stopped her from seeing the very clear signs that John was lying to her. Her preconceptions not only blinded her to the evidence, but meant she couldn't believe her daughters' warnings.

One constant frustration faced by nunchi ninjas, such as Jacquelyn and Terra, is that nobody believes them until it's too late. The clash between the mother and her daughters—which caused them to become estranged—was based on a disagreement over an age-old question: "Should you trust your first impressions, or is that unfair prejudice?"

If you think nunchi is just prejudice, reconsider and ask yourself instead what prejudices might be obscuring your nunchi.

First Impressions: Believe Them

People often suppress the wisdom of their first impressions because society tells us to be gracious and give everyone the benefit of the doubt, no matter what. Well, I'm here to tell you that society is wrong.

Civilization is only thousands of years old and your lived experience is likely only a few decades long; your survival instincts, by contrast, have evolved over literally millions of years and are woven into your DNA. Which do you think is more reliable?

I hear your objections. Telling people to trust their first impressions seems like an unraveling of a civilized upbringing. It's not politically correct. Isn't making snap judgments often due to racism, sexism, and other forms of bigotry?

Of course, bigotry is real. Of course, people often misperceive others as threatening based on unfair criteria such as race, class, religion, and sexual orientation. Let me be clear: that isn't your nunchi talking. It's bigotry. In fact, I would argue that nunchi is an *antidote* to bigotry, in that it asks you to be aware of your preconceptions at all times.

An unfair prejudice is one you stubbornly hold on to no matter what else is put before you. Prejudice is fixed, and does not adapt to changing information. But a nunchi-based first impression, on the other hand, is what you get when you switch on your nunchi before you do anything else, and let it do its magic.

Prejudice is often wrong. Nunchi rarely is.

To Quote Sherlock Holmes, "Data! Data! Data!"[7]

When you are truly getting to know a person or a work-place or a new situation, there is simply no substitute for lots of data. But there is no point in just collecting data before you form a nunchi-based first impression, as you may find yourself collecting the wrong data altogether.

What you need is a nunchi hypothesis, which your accu-mulated data will either prove or disprove.

Imagine you have started a new job, and you meet a colleague who tells you repeatedly how great and how successful he is, and how well regarded by your boss. At first glance, this colleague looks to be an unbearable show-off, and that might turn out to be accurate, but your nunchi-based impression might go a little further to ask why he feels he has to say such things to a new member of the team.

This is where you want to implement Nunchi Rule #3: If you just arrived, remember that everyone else has been there longer than you. Watch them to get information about this new job environment.

Perhaps you hear a random person comment in the office kitchenette, "Who the hell are all these new employees, taking all the coconut water and pistachios?" Hmm...So there were a bunch of new employees starting at once. Why? You begin to wonder whether Mr. Wonderful shares this resentment of the fresh blood. Maybe he assumed he would get your job and wants to put you in your place? Now you have a nunchi hypothesis! Don't jump to conclusions, but you can begin to gather the data that will allow you to determine how the company hierarchy works, and where your place in it, and your colleague's, might be. Watch how everyone treats you: are the old guard consistently stand-offish, whereas the newer employees are more open? Who is Mr. Wonderful lunching with? Do they act weird with you as well? Keep your mind fluid to new data and adapt accordingly. Don't get stuck following one theory just because it's convenient, or you may lose perspective and grossly misinterpret what you see. And don't ignore the possibility that the explanation is often boring: Mr. Wonderful might just be a show-off after all.

Nunchi is also one of the most powerful tools in your arsenal to combat a persistent villain in most people's life stories: denial.

Unfortunately, it is human nature to gather the wrong data intentionally so that you avoid heading toward inconvenient truths. If you meet someone devastatingly attractive, or if you are offered an opportunity that is too good to be true, you are likely to cherry-pick the data so that it supports whatever you desire. This is when you need to activate your nunchi discernment to look not just at what is happening, but why.

Shakespeare was rarely wrong about anything; listen to him. When you enter a room—be it a conference room, a party, or a family gathering—think of it as a stage. Everyone on the stage is part of the scene, whether they're interacting with the other players or not.

In a play, when a character enters the stage, action always follows. The new character, no matter how minor, signals some kind of change in where the scene is going.

This is true even when the person is not supposed to be there. Years ago, I was watching a play, and there was a scene in which a character was supposed to hold up a black dress and show it to her sister. But there was no dress. The prop guy had to sneak up and put the dress there, in the middle of the scene. He altered the viewing experience. During the interval, people weren't talking about the play, they were talking about the prop guy.

A nunchi ninja watches a room the way a theatergoer watches a play. Everyone in the room matters and affects the room's "climate," whether they're the life of the party or the wallflower, the host or the help. The room's story is not static. Your nunchi should not be static either. Stay aware of plot twists.

Let's say you meet someone at a party—Flavio, a charming and flirtatious man who introduces himself as a human rights lawyer. All signals so far suggest that Flavio is a person worth knowing, and you're intrigued. Half an hour into the chat, a woman marches up to Flavio and says, "Why are you here? Stay away from me." She leaves. Flavio says, "Ignore her. She's crazy."

This woman is a new player with new information, and you have to adapt. It is possible that the woman might indeed be "crazy"; on the other hand, you know that people who call others "crazy" are often suspect themselves. You don't have enough information yet to decide. But that doesn't mean you should ignore what you saw, just because it contradicts your initial eye-assessment that Flavio was an OK person.

There is no need to be rude to Flavio, but you will learn a lot more about him by *not* watching him too closely at this point. You should start to mingle, admire the books and furnishings, and watch Flavio from the corner of your eye to see how he interacts with others. Give him some distance to allow him to show who he really is. Is he pouting and sulking at being ignored by you? Flirting with everyone else? Following you? Making frequent trips to the toilet and returning with a runny nose and bloodshot eyes? There is a very good chance that you will have all the information you need by the end of the evening.

Nunchi might sound exhausting, but you know what's even more exhausting? Getting a restraining order.

In other words, an ounce of prevention is worth a pound of cure. You do not need to apologize for judging a person based on your nunchi. You do not need to prove to anyone that you have "earned" the right to decide for yourself whom you do and don't trust.

How Criminals Use Nunchi...and How You Can Use Your Nunchi to Spot Them

Nunchi is a powerful tool that, in the wrong hands, can be used for ill. Professional swindlers and imposters are all nunchi ninjas when it comes to reading people they've only just met.

One job that epitomizes using nunchi for ill is the storefront psychic in the U.S.—the kind with the neon signs, and the psychic trying to drag you in off the street or stuff brochures into your hand. Bob Nygaard, a retired New York police detective, now works as a private investigator in Florida, specializing in uncovering psychic scams. He's recovered millions for his clients and helped bring the psychics to justice. He explained how psychics use their nunchi: "One of the first things a psychic can see out the window is what kind of car you're driving," said Nygaard. "A Mercedes? An old jalopy? Then, when you get out of the car: are you walking with confidence? Do you look like you've been crying, like you got a bad diagnosis from the doctor? Then, upon meeting you: are you wearing a cross? If you're sitting across from an atheist, you're not going to say, 'God wanted us to meet today.' You will say, 'The universe wanted us to meet.'"

Nygaard emphasized the importance of recalibrating your assumptions based on new evidence. "When I got duped as a detective, it was when I judged something incorrectly because of assumptions I drew. You gotta keep an open mind, to all situations. When Sherlock Holmes solves a crime, how does he go about that? By keeping an open mind."

One bit of culture shock you may experience on your way to nunchi excellence is finding you are harshly judged for deciding you do not like someone who has not (yet) hit anyone or committed a crime or advocated genocide. It's shocking how many people feel that while you don't need to give a reason to like a person, you'd better have a reason for *not* liking them.

Remember: if your nunchi has done its due diligence and tells you someone is dangerous, or makes you uncomfortable, you do *not* have to "earn" the right to dislike that person.

Koreans aren't the world's most cynical people, but neither do they assume that everyone is acting with the best of motives. They reserve judgment and wait to see before deciding whether someone is trustworthy or likable.

That's why you need nunchi. First, empty your mind, and then let your nunchi do the work.

Priti was from a family where arranged marriages were common, though not mandatory. Her parents hired a matchmaker for her. They'd never force her to wed someone she didn't like. On the other hand, it was understood that she and a prospective groom would have to decide within a few weeks of meeting whether to get engaged. They could meet as many times as they wanted during that time, but speed mattered: the parents had used a matchmaker to find a husband for Priti, not a boyfriend to shack up with for years before deciding whether to marry or have kids. Picking a groom so quickly requires laser-focused nunchi based on limited data.

Priti had told the matchmaker that certain traits were nonnegotiable: any potential groom had to be tall, rich, and either an engineer or a doctor. But after meeting dozens of men fulfilling that description, and finding them all unlikable, her mother made an intriguing suggestion: why not tell the matchmaker that one out of five matches could be a "wild card"—someone of the matchmaker's choosing who might not tick all of Priti's boxes, but who could be a good match anyway.

You can guess what happened next. The first "wild card" was Amit, the shortest of the lot, and a lawyer to boot—a profession that Priti had originally said was off the table because she'd had a bad experience with a law-student boyfriend back in college. At first sight, Amit didn't give Priti butterflies in her stomach.

He didn't "sell himself." He was well-read and well-traveled but didn't tell her any hilarious stories. By the end of the meeting, she didn't really have a handle on him—because he had created an atmosphere of roundness and had not presented jagged edges to create that handle. She wouldn't be able to give him a funny nickname when telling her friends about Amit, unlike her other matches, whom she'd dubbed things like "Crocodile Briefcase" and "Mr. Golf."

Her takeaway from the meeting was just a gut feeling: it was the first time she'd met a potential groom who made her feel relaxed after the meeting and not anxious. At her mother's urging to give him a chance, Priti met with Amit several more times. She put aside her initial list of requirements and used her nunchi instead. As soon as she opened her mind, she noticed all kinds of qualities she didn't even realize she wanted: he was patient, considerate without expecting to be applauded for it, and a good listener. Fast forward a few years: married, happy, two amusing kids.

Beware of Overruling Your Nunchi

Nunchi has three major aspects: one is creating harmony; another is getting what you want; and the third is staying out of danger. I have found that many women are naturally good at the harmony part, and can be skilled at getting their needs met, but all too often women overrule their own nunchi instincts when it comes to the aspect of self-preservation.

I've noticed, particularly in the workplace, that women tend to know what's going on; they just don't trust their judgment—at least in the West. In Korea, nunchi is not considered a uniquely "feminine" trait, and Korean women are unashamed of trusting their intuition; furthermore, despite persistent sexist elements in Korean society, people in general are apt to respect female nunchi as much as they respect male nunchi.

Many women in the workplace tell themselves, "I'm wrong some of the time, therefore I am wrong all of the time." It's perverse. Even the most capable women do it. And sometimes this self-doubt can result in some career-damaging misjudgments.

Xenia is a news radio producer. A few years ago, she had to hire a new on-air host. She and two other senior members of staff interviewed one candidate, Sam, who seemed very well qualified for the job: he had a good demo tape, seemed charming, and understood the key millennial demographic. But during the interview process, Sam said a few things that raised Xenia's nunchi antennae.

For example, he asked out of nowhere, "Are your female employees paid the same as your male employees? Gender wage disparities really make me angry." Then later, unprompted, he told them: "My girlfriend is active in the pro-choice movement and so am I."

On the surface, it looked as though he was a feminist. But something about Sam rubbed Xenia the wrong way. Sam's comments made her think that he "doth protest too much." In addition, something about his body language made her think he was lying: every time he made one of his supposedly feminist statements, he stared fixedly at a spot on the table instead of looking at the interviewers.

Xenia didn't trust Sam, but the other interviewers thought she was being unfair for saying that he "seemed" like a liar, so she convinced herself that she was being unreasonable and they hired him.

Less than a year later, Xenia and a dozen others were out of a job due to Sam. A man who had been a guest on the show called the radio station's parent company to inform them that Sam had accosted his personal assistant while "guiding" her to the ladies' room. Once this story got out, two of Sam's female interns then informed HR that he had given an expense account to male interns but not to female interns. More stories of misconduct emerged. The show was suspended indefinitely.

Xenia is back on her feet now, but she really wishes she had trusted her nunchi and blocked Sam's hiring in the first place.

Don't take at face value what people are telling you; what's more important is what your senses are telling you.

The renowned psychologist and con expert Maria Konnikova recently became a successful professional poker player, and an expert on the "tell," or the way a player's behavior or demeanor can indicate their hand. She emphasizes that it's not what people think. She told me, "A lot of people love to stare you in the eyes and think they can get a tell off you. I'm much more careful to look at other kinds of behavior: the stories people are telling, consistencies and inconsistencies."

Konnikova gave an excellent piece of advice about anything you think is a so-called tell: "Data is only valuable in context." This recalls a nunchi principle we've already looked at: the unit of nunchi is the room. It's not all about you; it's not even about just your poker table.

This is why you must learn to trust your nunchi more than trust lists of physical "red flags" you may have read about. Your own intuition is your best guide on who you should trust.

Spotting "Stomach-Suckers"

Part and parcel of nunchi is quickly being able to readjust your reading of a person, room, or situation based on new information. Always remember that the room you entered half an hour ago is not the same room you are in now.

Why is it so important to be adaptable to change? Because most people can behave well in the short term. You have to pay attention to see if they can sustain it.

For a faker such as Dirty John, good behavior does not come naturally, and they can't keep it up for very long. Imagine that you're at a party and talking to someone really hot. You might instinctively suck in your stomach to appear thinner. How long can you do that for? Most people probably couldn't manage it for more than ten minutes at a time; it starts to become painful and hard to breathe. Maybe you can do it on and off for a whole day. But you cannot do it for any sustained period.

If you have good nunchi, you are able to spot when someone is, metaphorically speaking, sucking in their stomach. Depending on who it is and the severity of the fakery, you may laugh it off, you may file it away as a warning? for later, or you may decide that it's not worth the risk and put that person out of your life. Your perception of people has to be as fluid as the situation itself.

Nunchi helps us to discern the difference between when someone is stomach-sucking just to look a bit better (such as out of nerves in a job interview or on a first date), and when they are doing it in order to make a false impression because of bad intentions. Be aware of context—all of us are stomach-suckers sometimes.

You Will Know Malignant Narcissists by Their Lack of Nunchi

You will often have to use your nunchi to spot other people's *lack* of nunchi. I'm not talking about spotting the average no-nunchi clueless person, who is relatively harmless. But in my experience, people superlatively lacking in nunchi are often malignant narcissists.

True narcissists treat other people as nothing more than a means to an end; if others get hurt by their actions, the narcissist sees them as mere collateral damage. Narcissists don't have their social antennae up because they don't care to; they do not see other people as worthy of their consideration.

By the time you've recognized a malignant narcissist such as Dirty John, you may be pretty far in, so it's worth being able to spot these people as early as possible. Remember Nunchi Rule #1: Empty your mind. First, try to drop your preconceptions, and see people as they are and not as you hope they might be ("my future husband," "my last chance at love").

And second, observe their sense of humor. In my experience, one obvious sign of a narcissist is that they are convinced of their amazing sense of humor. I'm not talking about people who tell corny or unfunny "dad jokes." What the malignant narcissist does is get mad when no one finds the joke funny.

At a party, Odin was cracking lame jokes but no one was laughing. So he doubled down and made the jokes increasingly offensive to get attention. Someone responded uncomfortably, "I've heard better jokes." Anyone with nunchi would have heard this comment as it was intended—a polite invitation to be quiet—but Odin continued until he found himself without an audience, as everyone had left the room. Later Odin was heard complaining to his girlfriend, "My jokes are funny. *They're* the ones who have no sense of humor." Poor nunchi is one thing, but this level of no nunchi was a giant indication of true narcissism. Some months later it was revealed that Odin had conned his girlfriend out of a large sum of money.

In many cases, if someone gets disproportionately annoyed that no one laughs at their jokes, it may indicate that they have a preternatural desire to be liked *regardless of their actions*, namely that they are a narcissist. Run away.

The danger of narcissists is one reason why I emphasize nunchi over empathy. Nunchi can keep you safe from narcissists, while empathy will get you buried deeper and deeper. In fact, as it's often been said, narcissists are naturally drawn to empaths, because the empath is constantly putting themselves in the narcissist's shoes, to the point of total self-effacement.

By contrast, nunchi allows you to try to understand what the other person is feeling or thinking *without losing your footing*. The best way to get out is to get out early.

How to See a Person for Who They Are

So how do you get to know someone, with wisdom and accuracy? The person will give you all the information you need, whether he or she realizes it or not.

If, soon after meeting someone, you begin to think, "I'm not sure about this person," that is your first clue that things may not be as they seem. Your nunchi is suggesting that you collect the data to support this first impression. There are a few immediate steps you can take, all of which are perfectly socially acceptable, and no one will be any the wiser.

Step 1: Return to Nunchi Rule #1, and empty your mind

How you go about this is different for everyone, and it might take you time to learn what works for you. When I was a kid and was taking part in piano competitions, as soon as I sat at the piano, I'd say to myself, "I'm not here." Euny the person is absent; only Euny the pianist is present. I still do this in social situations and job interviews—any time when I need a moment of clarity.

For the vast majority of people, the best shortcut to centering yourself is to breathe deeply. It doesn't matter whether you do it in front of everyone or duck into the bathroom; just do it. I know telling people to breathe is a cliché, but that doesn't mean it's invalid. As I'm sure you've been told many times, deep breaths reduce anxiety and clear the head. This creates a clean path for your nunchi to work.

Two very effective breathing techniques are the 4-7-8 and box breathing. Both techniques will trigger your brain to slow down the release of cortisol—the stress hormone.

The 4-7-8 technique was popularized by wellness expert Dr. Andrew Weil; the numbers represent breath counts. Inhaling is done through the nose, exhaling through the mouth. To use this technique, inhale for four counts, hold your breath for seven counts, and exhale for eight counts;

repeat. Why the weird irregular numbers? Precisely because they're irregular, you have to concentrate on counting. This distracts the mind while the oxygen relaxes it.

Box breathing is so called because it is done in four stages. Inhale for four counts, hold for four counts, exhale for four counts, hold for four counts; repeat.

If you're already engaged in conversation, just do one abbreviated version: breathe in for four counts, then out for four counts, while the other person is talking. Just once is fine.

If you're feeling too much anxiety for breathing to work, go to the bathroom and run ice-cold water over your wrists for five minutes (it's better to dip your face in water, but this could ruin your makeup). Some people believe this triggers what is known as the "mammalian dive response," which is to say that if you trick your instinctive brain into thinking you are going underwater, your body responds by slowing down to prevent drowning.

Step 2: Pay careful, excruciating attention to how the person wants to be greeted

Remember Nunchi Rule #6: read between the lines—from the very first moment you lay eyes on someone, before you even say hi. That initial greeting matters a lot. Don't assume that everyone does exactly what you and your friends do.

The minute you forget this can be the minute someone stops wanting to get to know you.

I know of several instances where someone was trying to be formal when meeting a friend's extended family, only to be met by a crushing bear hug and the comment, "Sorry, we're a family of huggers." Why do people do this? Many people are not comfortable hugging. In essence, you are saying, "We outnumber you and thus are using a display of force."

When meeting *anyone* for the first time, watch them to see how they expect to be greeted. Do they look as though they're planning to bow, shake your hand, do the French *bises* (cheek kisses), or—believe it or not—none of the above? Don't hug your colleague's wife/husband, only to find that the couple are from a culture where a man and woman who are not spouses are not supposed to touch each other, or you'll discover that you've basically committed assault in their eyes.

Regardless of cultural background, some people don't like to be touched—never assume that they do. One famous American investor is extremely germophobic, the sort who uses Kleenex to open doorknobs because he doesn't want to touch anything with his bare hands. Even if you hadn't heard the gossip about him, a nunchi ninja would notice that in meetings this investor always has his hands clasped tightly behind his back to avoid handshakes, and that although his closest friends may be standing around him, they are still a good four feet away.

Don't colonize people. Every person has their own idea of what the appropriate distance is between two people, and they will communicate this *extremely clearly* to you in their behavior. Be discerning.

Step 3: Turn down the volume to "hear" what a person's really all about

Don't just think about the words coming out of people's mouths—think about the overall context, think about their biases and values.

Have you ever watched television with the volume off—perhaps because you took a phone call but didn't want to miss the exciting climax of your favorite show? You may have noticed that you can often guess exactly what is happening in the plot even without the sound. If a couple is rolling around in bed and then sit up in horror as a man walks into the bedroom, it suggests that the couple may be having an illicit affair. If a murder suspect in an Agatha Christie mystery starts running from the parlor, it means the detective has identified them as the murderer.

Nunchi is the ability to see what's going on, based on nonverbal cues: facial gestures and body language being the big ones.

Maybe a colleague has corrected your errors quietly and with a patient tone of voice, but you can tell from their tense shoulders and nonblinking eyes that they're furious. The matter is therefore much more serious than they're letting on, and you'd better snap to it.

Paying attention to what is *not* being said can tell you a great deal more than listening to every word that *is* being said.

Following these steps won't give you an immediate "aha, case closed, I have comprehensively gotten a handle on this person" moment. You may simply realize you need more information in areas X, Y, and Z before making any further assumptions. Just the act of gathering data for yourself is still an excellent use of nunchi.

Context and Nunchi

We all like to think we're far too sophisticated to believe that first impressions count. We're modern, we're woke, we know about unconscious bias, and we wouldn't dream of judging someone based on their appearance. Except we do it all the time.

People learn by associating new experiences with previous ones: if new Situation X has one or two superficial things in common with old Situation Y, our brains make us believe that the two experiences are likely to be *identical* in every way. This is useful in remembering that hornets sometimes sting, but it's far less useful when it comes to judging people.

In a 2018 study published by the U.S. National Academy of Sciences,[8] researchers showed a group of people numerous photos of strangers and asked them to choose which ones looked trustworthy. What the test subjects were *not* told was that some of the images were just slightly photoshopped versions of the same face. Guess what? Once the test takers deemed certain faces were trustworthy, they kept selecting the doctored variations of the exact same faces.

Whether it's feeling kinship with a stranger because they're wearing the same shoes as you, or shifting uncomfortably away from someone on public transport because they smell bad, or not wanting to sit next to the guy wearing a political T-shirt that you disagree with, you're judging, and most of the time you're not even aware of it. And everyone's doing it to you, too.

Maya has a T-shirt she adores, on which is stenciled a quote from Rolling Stones drummer Keith Richards: "I've never had a problem with drugs. I've had a problem with the police." Maya doesn't do drugs at all, nor has she ever had brushes with the police; it's an ironic T-shirt. In her hip Brooklyn neighborhood, she's used to people stopping to laugh about it. But when Maya wore the shirt to the airport for an international flight, she found the security officers had a totally different attitude. They took her aside for a search and asked about her reasons for traveling.

Sure, the security officers overreacted to a pretty innocuous T-shirt, but Maya had not considered something that is key in acting with good nunchi: context. There was nothing wrong with her T-shirt, other than it presented a jagged edge for others to grab hold of. That jagged edge was cute and ironic in Brooklyn, but it made her security check last longer. No one wants that. Make a statement if you want, obviously, but be aware of context before you make one by accident.

Context is a reminder of one of the unspoken rules of nunchi: it's not all about you. People are picking up on signals all the time, consciously and unconsciously. Beware of giving them an edge to grab hold of.

Reading context can make or break politicians. Two major French leaders were received very differently during their respective visits to the annual agricultural show in Paris. Jacques Chirac greeted the farmers warmly and rhapsodized over their cheeses and beer samples as if every bite were ambrosia. He understood his context. The farmers and vintners' chests puffed with pride, and he was very popular at the event.

However Nicolas Sarkozy approached the farmers as if he were haggling with them, wagging his finger sternly and lecturing them about European Union dairy prices. One vexed man angrily refused to shake Sarkozy's hand, and the politician lost his cool and told the man, "Piss off, cretin!" (*"Casse-toi, pauv' con"*). It was a public-relations disaster.

This was not merely rudeness on Sarkozy's part; it was an example of terrible nunchi in that he did not take the context of the event into account. If he'd picked on someone his own size and snapped at a corrupt oil oligarch, he'd have been a media darling. But he should not have lost his temper at an ordinary citizen, at the agricultural fair of all places—the most wholesome, salt-of-the-earth event imaginable. The public and media were merciless. If you are famous, you lose the luxury of ignoring context, especially nowadays when a gaffe caught on video can go viral.

Nunchi asks you to find a balance between being who you are, and moving through the world in a manner that is most likely to get you where you want to go with the least amount of friction for everyone (including you).

Making a Good First Impression

There are times when we are particularly anxious that our first impression is a good one: meeting a partner's parents for the first time, for example, or being introduced to someone who might be helpful in your career. Standard Western advice for such situations suggests focusing on yourself: give a firm handshake, look people in the eye, speak in a strong and confident tone of voice. Nunchi suggests the opposite: take the focus off yourself in order to see more clearly what the situation demands and let your behavior be led by the person whose good opinion you need.

Much of this can be done by mirroring, which is something we all do subconsciously and which, as we saw in the North–South Korea summit, can be a way of demonstrating affinity. Mirroring means reflecting someone's gestures, or tone of voice, or even the words they use—not in a creepy *Single White Female* style, but with restraint.

People will find they are well disposed to you without even knowing why, because you appear to be so in tune with them and their thoughts.

Think of Clyde, meeting his girlfriend's parents for the first time. At the restaurant, Clyde sees there is a special dish on the menu: his favorite pasta with fresh white truffles flown in from Elba. It comes at a hefty price, but truffle season is short, and Clyde doesn't want to miss out. No-nunchi Clyde orders the truffled pasta, and then is mortified when he sees his girlfriend's parents, who are paying for the meal, select the cheapest dishes on the menu. If Clyde had used his nunchi he would have asked his girlfriend's parents what dishes they recommended from the menu, or would have insisted they order first. This would have given him an indication of whether they were going all-out with lobster and other expensive dishes, or whether their budget was more modest. Being guided by the person you wish to impress will rarely let you down.

Mirroring someone's tone of voice can be a very nunchi-ful way to make an immediate connection too, as long as you do it carefully and don't appear to be mimicking. This means matching their tone, whether that is excited or angry or quiet. You are making an effort to meet them where they are, instead of imposing your own tone on them.

Take Dan, for example, a vacuum cleaner salesman who often has to deal with disgruntled customers coming into the shop demanding refunds or replacements. Dan's goal is to neutralize the situation as quickly as possible, so that the customer leaves feeling happy that he has offered them a good solution. When he first began the job, he would ask the angry customers to "Calm down" before offering them a refund or replacement, but he soon discovered this tactic only enraged them more, as they felt he was dismissing their legitimate concerns. Now Dan approaches the situation like this:

CUSTOMER: I bought this from you last week and it's already broken!

DAN: What? That is terrible! You must be so annoyed.

CUSTOMER: I *am* annoyed, I've had to come all the way back to the store, it's miles out of my way and I had to leave work early.

DAN: I'd be furious too, this really shouldn't happen. Especially when the machine is brand new.

CUSTOMER: It really shouldn't.

DAN: I'm so sorry we've let you down. How can we make it up to you?

CUSTOMER: I want you to replace it free of charge.

DAN: I quite understand. Let me see what we can do for you.

By matching the tone of the angry customer, Dan meets them on their level. They feel their concerns are heard and understood. They lose their urge to escalate the argument because they believe that both parties are already on the same page. This allows Dan to bring the conversation to a resolution much more quickly than if he said (as he sometimes thinks), "Relax, man, it's only a vacuum cleaner."

Notice also that Dan didn't actually agree to replace the vacuum free of charge (he might not be allowed to). He also didn't blame his colleagues and he didn't disparage the brand of vacuum cleaner. When you have nunchi you can get on someone's wavelength without making them promises or throwing everyone else under the bus.

When making a first impression is really important to you, here's some counterintuitive-sounding advice: thinking of yourself less, and focusing on everyone *but* yourself, may be the best way to find the good connection that you seek.

Asking Questions

We're often told that asking questions is a good thing to do when we first meet people—and, of course, it is far better than offering a monologue about yourself. But it is possible to believe you're using your nunchi, while doing the opposite. When you ask questions, you are focusing on the other person; but if you fail to notice their response to the questions, you are not exercising good nunchi. What if your questions make the person uncomfortable? Are they blushing or stammering or looking around the room? Are they narrowing their eyes with anger? Not everyone is going to say directly, "Well, that's rude," but their body language will say it for them, and you need to read those signs.

To give a personal example, the following conversation will make most Asians living outside of Asia extricate themselves from the interaction as soon as possible and scorch the earth behind them.

NO-NUNCHI: Where are you from?

DIASPORIC ASIAN: I'm from [Auckland/Birmingham/
                          Paris/other cities in predominantly
                          non-Asian nations]

NO-NUNCHI: No, but where are you *really* from? Like,
                          your parents, what country are they
                          from?

If you ask this sort of question, what are you thinking?

Basically, the no-nunchi person has a set of correct answers in mind (China, Japan, Korea, etc.) and if you don't name one of those, you get the red buzzer as far as they are concerned.

I am astonished at the number of times I've had to explain why this line of questioning is bad; on the other hand, blow-dryers still have warning stickers that tell you not to use them in the bath, so I reckon some things have to be spelled out: unless you're an international agent hunting down a master of disguise, please don't ask a follow-up question that is preceded by "No, you're not!" or suggest in any way that the other party's answer lacks credulity. Accept the answer you are given and move on with no further questions.

"But I was just interested!" is no defense in this situation. Your inquisitiveness does not overrule the other party's right to answer, or *not* answer, your questions as they see fit. See also, "When are you planning on getting married/having children/losing that baby weight?"

Don't forget Nunchi Rule #4: Never pass up a good opportunity to shut up.

QUICK QUIZ: FINDING THE DECISION-MAKER

You are an account executive for a company that sells ergonomic, vegan, cruelty-free espresso machines. When you're already home from work one evening, your boss calls to tell you that you'd better rush to some cocktail event in town, because it's being hosted by the world's second-biggest cruelty-free coffee-shop chain. The bad news: you've already missed some of the event, and by the time you get there, there will be less than half an hour remaining. How do you maximize your time once you arrive?

A.   Give your printed sales materials to everyone you see.

B.   Approach the oldest, whitest, baldest man.

C.   Approach the best-dressed person.

D.   Approach the loudest person.

E.   Approach the person surrounded by the most people.

Correct answer: trick question. All the answers are wrong, as you do not have nearly enough information. In the absence of context, all five answers represent unfounded assumptions about who the decision maker is, and are not nunchi-based judgments. In some cases, the answer will be A) Give your printed sales materials to everyone you see—but this will depend on the business culture. In many parts of the world, you don't make brazen requests to people you have just met; rather, you get their card and contact them the next day to set up a meeting. Of course, you probably googled the company and their team while in the taxi, but if you still don't recognize anyone at the cocktail event, take a few more minutes to stand around and sip your drink, or stand by a place with a lot of foot traffic. Eye-measure the room. Even if your time is limited—*especially* if your time is limited—you have to have a plan before you start talking to people.

If you don't know who the decision maker is, you don't have to give yourself brain fever trying to guess, based on limited clues such as clothing and voice. Instead, look for the helpers.

In business, and in life in general, you need to find the most helpful person, not necessarily the highest-ranking person.

At corporate events such as a promotional cocktail party, there will usually be a person pouring wine, either professional bartenders or "lowly" interns—people that a no-nunchi person might dismiss as being "not important enough" to bother with. But *you* are not a no-nunchi person; you are well on your way to becoming a nunchi ninja. You know that if someone has been asked to serve drinks, it's also their job to be polite and helpful. Ask that person point-blank who the decision maker is and how best to approach them. They might not know, but they may at least introduce you to their boss, and so on, till you reach someone who can make that introduction with no further intermediaries.

I'm sure you've heard people say that you should never do business with anyone who is rude to waitstaff. This is not only kind; it's also very practical. More often than not, the seemingly "insignificant" staff are the ones who are omniscient. Think about the one person in your office who seems to know everything that's going on and is allowed to interrupt the CEO with impunity: very often, it's the front-desk receptionist or the office manager. A nunchi ninja knows that you need these people on your side.

CHAPTER 7

Nunchi and Relationships

In seventh grade at my school in Seoul, the social studies textbook opened with a quote from Aristotle: "Man is by nature a political animal." I remember this vividly because the text was accompanied by a photograph of ants, and I hate ants. The chapter went on to explain that, despite living in groups, ants don't have to be political to survive, because they operate solely on instinct.

The fact that a Korean school textbook would begin in this way is a testament to how much Korean culture values seeing oneself as part of a larger organism. Korea's Confucian roots, which still run through the country's surface, are based on the belief that every member serve a role that interlocks with everyone else. Deviating from your role disrupts the whole and, if everyone were to do it, society would disintegrate.

That said, Confucianism is impractical in modern capitalist life, which is why much of it has fallen by the wayside in Korea. But it is interesting how closely old Korean society was aligned with the ancient Greek philosophers, specifically the belief that humans live in a group because they cannot survive outside it. Again, from Aristotle: "the complete community... comes to be for the sake of life, and exists for the sake of the good life."

The good life.

Isn't that what we all want? I studied philosophy as an undergraduate, in pursuit of an answer to the question of where the good life was to be found. It turned out to be sort of a *Wizard of Oz* situation—the answer was in my own backyard, in my own upbringing: the good life comes about in large part through nunchi, and the observation of others.

Many modern people would bristle at this concept. Some version of "I just gotta be me" has been the battle cry of the last several, individualistic generations—my generation was encapsulated by complaint rock by bands like Nirvana. These days, the motto seems to be a perkier "You do you."

Well, I think it's obvious to all sentient twenty-first-century beings that several generations of this self-centered mentality have come back to bite us. Some commentators suggest that late-stage capitalism is in the process of collapsing in on itself—resulting in such phenomena as worsening wealth disparities and making the earth increasingly uninhabitable. I think that people of all political persuasions are finally admitting that we need to get along, and consider others, in order for civilization to survive. We were wrong. Aristotle was right.

Misanthropes rejoice: I promise you don't have to like people at all in order to get along with them. If you exercise good nunchi, you will create that social roundness we talked about, which makes it easier for you to drift in and out of conversations, if that's what you want. Hermits often make the mistake of hoping that if they act prickly, people will leave them in peace. In fact, it is usually the opposite.

Let's say you don't like being around people. If that's the case, you probably want to get in and out of the post office quickly. If the postal worker says, "Oh, hi again! How's work these days?," which response is likely to get you out faster: "Oh, great, thanks" or "How is that any of your business?" With the latter, you're just hurting yourself. Roundness makes interactions frictionless, so you can run back to your cave if you want. You can be as invisible or as visible as you desire. It's the people who are bad at nunchi who are always disturbing their environment and creating jagged edges with people.

Let nunchi help you smooth the edges of social interactions. Regardless of who you are, or how complicated your relationships, nunchi can help you move through life in a way that feels harmonious for you and everyone you encounter.

Nunchi and Dating

They say there are no atheists in foxholes; similarly, no one doubts the power of nunchi when it comes to dating. This is particularly true in the early stages of getting to know someone.

Online dating has made it commonplace to go out with someone about whom you know less than a random stranger on your morning commute. In many cases you will need to discern as quickly as possible whether the person you are meeting is dangerous (especially necessary if you are a woman) or worthy of your trust.

You cannot rely on the words coming out of a person's mouth or what you read on their online profile. You have to use your nunchi.

People on dates spend far too much energy trying to control the impression they are making on the other person, leaving no mental room to use their powers of nunchi. That's a pity, since they're cheating themselves out of a valuable opportunity to read the other person.

If you pay attention to reading the other person—better yet, the whole room—your focus moves away from yourself, which has a magically calming effect. Who doesn't want to dissipate the nervousness we all inevitably feel on a first date? Focus on the room and you will feel more relaxed immediately.

Asking questions is always great on a first date, not just because it's poor nunchi to talk about yourself the whole time, but because people's answers can give away a lot more than they intend.

Is your date avoiding answering all questions about family because he is an orphan, or because he has just buried them all in his backyard? He's unlikely to tell you either on first meeting, but you might at least learn that there is some issue about his family that makes him uncomfortable.

Is your date vague about where she lives because she doesn't want to give away too much personal information to a stranger or because she has a husband and two kids at home? Again, her actual words are not going to be the giveaway here, but on a first date you are looking out for both what is said and what is not said.

It is also helpful to gauge your date's nunchi skills. How do they relate to the room themselves? If the wine they wanted isn't available, for example, do they make a big deal of it or do they just choose another one? Are they friendly and approachable to others, or closed off and guarded? Don't just judge the way they behave with you, but assess the way they behave with everyone.

Tonya went on a date with Alex, a guy she'd met at her yoga class. He was incredibly good-looking and super-fit, and spoke convincingly of his deep spiritual practice and journey toward enlightenment. Yet in between stories about how his ashram stays taught him inner peace and patience, Alex became very *im*patient whenever the waitress didn't come straight away, making remarks like, "What's taking them so long, are they flying in their beef from New Zealand?" and "Are the waitstaff on strike?" This mismatch between his words and his actions made Tonya decide against a second date.

Loads of relationship experts will tell you to investigate why a potential love interest broke up with their past partners. If they blame their exes for everything, then this is a red flag, blah blah blah. If only it were that simple. Categorical advice like that can be a useful guide, but nothing beats your own discernment, and no one else knows your experiences. Everyone has his or her own warning signals; some might be sound, and some might be irrational, but that's for you and your nunchi to decide.

Trust yourself.

Finding Mr./Ms. Right

So how *do* you find the right partner? Some friends will tell you to make a list of must-haves that you're looking for, and not to budge from these. Others will tell you the exact opposite—that you have to throw your must-haves out of the window or you will remain alone for ever. The reality is that neither of those extremes applies to all situations. It would be so much easier if you could just follow rules set in stone, but finding a mate is as complicated as you are, multiplied by how complicated everyone else is.

Nunchi is the middle path here. You neither have to drop all your standards nor enforce them unrealistically; what's important is that you are discerning and adaptable. Gather data, and for pity's sake don't ignore new data just because it tells you what you don't want to hear.

Again, *Pride and Prejudice* offers the best lessons in the world on the importance of nunchi when seeking a potential mate. After all, both pride and prejudice are inhibitors to judgment. The "pride" of the title refers to the initial snobbery of Mr. Darcy, who deems the Bennet family to be beneath his station. The "prejudice" is that of Lizzy Bennet, whose mind is shut when it comes to Darcy because she overheard him tell a friend that she is "not handsome enough to tempt me." Admittedly, that was a dick move on his part, but when we learn more of his character, we realize that he obviously didn't mean it and was probably just trying to seem cool in front of his friends.

For most of the book, Darcy and Elizabeth can't be a couple because they each have inflexible negative views of the other. But then various life emergencies (illness, family scandals) force them to interact with each other and break the barriers to work toward common goals. They open their minds, observe how the other person behaves in different situations, and adapt accordingly to this new data. They each do something that is horribly difficult for them: they admit that their pride and prejudice might have been blocking their ability to discern. Without this late-found nunchi, they might not have had their happily ever after.

Nunchi-ful Partnerships

Think of the couples that you love to be around, and I will bet they are couples with good nunchi. Couples who are considerate of each other's feelings, and who can anticipate each other's needs, have a way of spreading those good and thoughtful vibes to others. We all want to spend more time with people like this. The opposite is true for couples with poor nunchi, who either do not see or do not care about their partner's needs. These are the couples whom everyone dreads having around. And as for being in a relationship like this? Having a partner who can't read between the lines to understand how you are feeling, how their words and actions affect you, or what you most need at a given time? Heartbreaking.

Now, I know that many relationship experts would dismiss nunchi and tell you exactly the opposite—that it's not your partner's job to read your mind, and that the onus is on you to express your needs clearly and calmly.

If only it were that simple! Unfortunately, this advice neglects the realities of human nature. Feelings are often complicated and not fully understood even by the person having them.

It's no one's fault, really. Conventionally, women were taught not to appear needy by asking for affection; while men were taught to believe that they shouldn't express feelings like shame or sadness.

Nunchi is pragmatic, in that it recognizes there is nothing you can do about the way you or your partner were raised. There is also nothing you can do to force another person to exercise their nunchi and become more considerate. Nunchi asks you to read the room as it is, rather than as you wish it was.

The only thing you can control is your own nunchi. Listen to your partner: if they're telling a boring story, use the nunchi ninja technique of mentally summarizing what they have just said. And listen not just on a verbal level, but also consider the whole scene: are they telling this boring story because they feel unheard at work or elsewhere? Is the story boring because the real details are too painful to communicate directly? Try asking them about their day before you launch into stories of your own. Show them the consideration that you wish they showed toward you.

You may find, to your great surprise, that improving your own nunchi will cause your partner to start improving theirs. Your nunchi will beget greater understanding, which makes your partner feel safer, which gives them the emotional freedom to pay attention to you as well. If you still find you are the only one demonstrating care and attention, you may have a compatibility problem that is beyond the scope of nunchi to fix.

We all want to feel that we are seen and heard in our closest relationships. Nunchi can bridge the divide between two people in subtle ways that reap big rewards.

Using Nunchi for Clashing Communication Styles

Do you remember as a teenager, when wanting to ask a big favor, like whether you could go to a concert, you'd actively put up your antennae to suss out when your parents were in a good mood? Even a very young child will notice that Mom is grumpy before she has her morning coffee or that Dad will agree to anything if you ask him while he's watching his favorite show, for which he needs absolute silence from you. In school, my classmate worked out that if she got bad marks, the best time to mention them was between the hours of seven and nine in the evening, when Korean television always ran slapstick variety shows.

For some reason, people throw all this valuable learning out of the window when they become adults. They think all that circumspection and gauging of mood are behind them, now that they're intelligent and mature, and everyone can simply use their words. But the reality is that the number of adults who don't feel comfortable communicating directly far outnumbers those who do. Many well-adjusted adults find that after moving in with a spouse or partner they somehow forget how to "use their words" and revert to the more indirect communication patterns of their childhood.

The spouse you thought was brash and fearless may start tiptoeing around you and become hesitant to tell you their thoughts and feelings, without even realizing it. If you are living with someone who has "regressed," you may find this frustrating. Try to find your compassion—and your nunchi.

Obviously, life would be so much simpler if your partner were to say "I'm cold" instead of "Are you cold?" as a way of feeling out whether it's OK to turn up the heat. But they might have been raised in a home where they were not allowed to express discomfort, where even a simple statement like "I'm cold" was considered selfish and annoying.

If your partner is prone to an indirect style of communication, the onus is on you and your nunchi to be aware of this and to adapt your behavior before you yell at them about fixing theirs.

Let's say you are walking around town and your partner Sheila is starting to get irritable. You've known her long enough to realize this happens when her blood sugar has dropped.

YOU: Dammit, Sheila, why didn't you say you were hungry? We just passed like seven restaurants and you didn't say anything.

SHEILA: I thought it was obvious. Couldn't you tell? Plus I told you an hour ago that I was tired.

YOU: Right, you said *tired*, not hungry, so that's why I got us those coffees! Hungry and tired are not the same thing!

SHEILA: When my blood sugar gets low, I get tired and hungry, so actually, Einstein, they *are* the same thing.

And so on. Couples who have this kind of argument tend to have it ALL THE TIME, to the annoyance of everyone around them. You have a choice: you could keep repeating this exchange every time you leave the house. Or you could use your nunchi and try to break the cycle.

Yes, Sheila really should say things more literally: if she's hungry, she should use the word "hungry," especially if she has a blood sugar problem. But she may never change, and you can't control her. Focus on your own nunchi, your own communication.

Keep in mind Nunchi Rule #6: Read between the lines. People don't always say what they are thinking, and that's their prerogative. Sheila's words are not coming out of a computer, and they're not a random Twitter message from an anonymous stranger. You've got plenty of context to go on, including the fact that you know she doesn't communicate directly.

You probably think I'm going to suggest that you pay attention to Sheila's body language every time you go out, to see if she needs to eat. But not in this case; when someone has a chronic problem like low blood sugar, monitoring them is not practical.

Instead, I recommend you ask Sheila questions that are based not on *whether* she wants to eat, but *when*. Next time you go out, bring up the question of food immediately when you step out of the door. You could say, "There's a new Indian place on York Street, and nearby there's pizza and all kinds of street vendors selling roasted chestnuts. Let me know *when you decide which restaurant you want*."

So what did you accomplish here? In the previous scenario—the recurring shouting match—you told Sheila it was her responsibility to tell you when she is hungry. But in the second scenario, by telling her to let you know *which restaurant* she has picked, you are shifting the action to one she is more comfortable with.

Even if your partner never changes, using your nunchi will always lighten the atmosphere between the two of you.

The Gallantry of Nunchi

There is a Korean children's book of poetry called *The Fart with No Nunchi*.[9] The cover art, a masterpiece, shows a naïf-art drawing of a boy with ochre-colored smoke coming out of his bum while two other boys scream and run. The book's title comes from the book's main poem: four stanzas from the point of view of a child playing outdoors with his pal Joonsang. Suddenly, Joonsang farts loudly. The fart has no nunchi—it came out without consideration of others. But the child narrator has excellent nunchi, and reacts immediately. "I quickly start counting the ants [on the ground]," he tells us, "and then, so does Joonsang. One ant, two ants, three . . . I stifle a laugh while Joonsang's face turns red." The narrator has allowed Joonsang to save face and avoid interruption of play. He created a round environment, in other words.

What the nameless child narrator does is an act of nunchi gallantry. This story illustrates one of the great things about nunchi: you can do it without drawing attention to it. In fact, discretion is the better part of nunchi.

You can be Joonsang's friend in your everyday life. Not just when someone farts, but if someone is being put on the spot.

For example, your friend Tom comes to a party alone because he's recently separated from his wife. You're the only one who knows this. Karen goes up to Tom and asks obliviously, "Hey, where's your better half?" A real nunchi ninja realizes that several other people will probably ask about Tom's wife. Instead of whispering the news to everyone and causing uncomfortable gossip, you suggest to Tom and a few others that they engage in an activity that requires concentration and minimal personal chatter. Chess, charades, poker, a strategy game, even badminton. Roundness reinstated without drawing any further attention to Tom's situation.

Many friends assume that they're so close they needn't read between the lines when their friend says something to them. False. You should use nunchi with friends, meaning that you should take into account not just their words, but their upbringing and changed life circumstances. A few years ago, I started knitting up a storm. I asked my friend Charlotte what her daughter Emily's favorite color was, because I wanted to knit the girl a shawl. I sent a photo of a shawl I'd previously made. A few days later, Charlotte replied, "I didn't know you were a knitter these days! That's a pretty shawl; so skillful!" Very pleasant, but notice the omission: she did not say that I should knit a shawl for Emily. That tact displayed excellent nunchi on her part. The nunchi on my part was that I didn't knit the shawl.

In my mind's eye, Emily was eternally four years old, so I had forgotten that she was now a preteen. No child that age would ever be caught dead wearing a handmade shawl.

It's not Charlotte's job to tell me, "I showed Emily the picture you sent and she said, 'Hell to the no'"; it would go against Charlotte's upbringing to create awkwardness. It's my job to read between the lines. If I'd insisted on making the shawl for Emily, I'd be putting the child in the excruciating position of having to wear it every time I saw her. (A note to craftsy people in general: it hurts me to say this, but please exercise nunchi when gifting people your creations. Otherwise, you are creating an obligation for them to display your doilies!)

People may not even notice your best nunchi, and that is a sign that you are becoming truly skilled.

Nunchi and Relatives, or Using Your Nunchi to Survive the Holidays

Everyone has potential explosive areas with one or more family members. It can be very hard to change your dynamic with a person you've known for a long time. Even if you have all evolved and matured, there is always potential for an explosion if some of you are acid and some are base. You cannot change your essential differences, but with practice you can use nunchi to weather them.

First, don't lie to yourself: you know exactly when a sensitive topic will trigger a fight with a family member or loved one, because you've likely had the same argument thousands of times before. Use your nunchi to sense tremors underfoot before anyone else does, and this time, do something different. And do that different thing over and over again until it becomes a habit. Please don't act like you're in a Greek tragedy: you can break the cycle and you are not doomed to have the same fight in perpetuity as if you're a puppet of the gods. As my psychiatrist likes to say, "You don't have to show up to every fight to which you're invited."

When it comes to dealing with family, the nunchi you use should mostly be on *yourself*. Are you falling into old, toxic patterns that always yield the same shitty result? For example, are you always trying to play mediator, forcing feuding family members to "hug it out"? If so, ask yourself what your own motives are for doing this, and be honest. Is it because you enjoy being the center of attention so badly that you're even willing to jump into a boxing ring? Is it because you have always been the "saintly" one in the family and are trying to play that role again? Upon reflection, you may realize that you are doing the right thing after all, but at least choose that role deliberately and not by default, as if you're stuck in a computer loop.

Unpopular opinion: if you find yourself in a social dynamic that requires preternatural amounts of nunchi on your part—be it among colleagues, friends, loved ones, or family—you should consider removing yourself from that dynamic for good. Nunchi, like money and energy, is in finite supply. If you continually use it to remedy an irremediable situation, you will find yourself lacking in resources for other areas of your life.

Mrs. Ramsay: A Model of Discreet Nunchi

An example of the low-profile, quiet nunchi expert is the character of Mrs. Ramsay from Virginia Woolf's novel *To the Lighthouse*. She's a consummate hostess, but not because she makes sparkling conversation or greets her guests with a signature cocktail. She knows that all she has to do to make a room fill with love and laughter is to light the dining room candles. The glow draws everyone together. The room transforms, as if by magic, from contentious and snippy to unified and warm. The discord both inside and outside the house disappears. "Some change at once went through them all . . . and they were all conscious of making a party together in a hollow, on an island; had their common cause against that fluidity out there."

Can you think of a Mrs. Ramsay in your life, past or present? I bet you can. If not, you can be Mrs. Ramsay yourself. In that one gesture of lighting the candles, she changed the room's "climate" and in so doing became a better wife, mother, hostess, and friend. All without saying a word.

Rich or poor, dominant culture or minority, privileged or not, gay or straight, male, female, and everything in between, you can do the equivalent of lighting a candle.

For example, if you're with a group of friends and they're all embarrassing Joanie and Michael with questions about why they haven't got engaged yet after five years of dating, you might be tempted to say, "Guys, leave them alone." But that would just draw more attention to the couple's embarrassment and sour the whole tone of the gathering. The friends might even resent Joanie and Michael for making them feel guilty about their actions.

It would be far better for you to change the subject to something on which everyone has an opinion, so they'll immediately want to dive in. Bringing up the latest crazy *Game of Thrones* fan theories is usually great for that. The more preposterous, the better: "I have a feeling that we'll find out the whole story is just a fever dream in the spin-off series from the point of view of a mushroom." Everyone will be so busy making fun of you they'll forget to persecute Joanie and Michael, and you'll have restored good feelings.

> ### QUICK QUIZ

Your friend farts loudly at dinner. What do you do?

A. Say, "New rule: no cruciferous vegetables within seventy-two hours of coming to my house."

B. Say, "It's not you, it's the chair, it's got some weird loose upholstery and it makes that noise when someone sits on it."

C. Pin the fart on someone you don't like.

D. Think of a diverting question on an unrelated topic for everyone to answer, e.g. "Can you remind me who wanted red wine and who wanted white? I need to know how many bottles to open."

E. Do nothing.

Correct answer: D. Asking something, or suggesting an activity, that requires everyone to participate and shift focus even for a second is the nunchi-ninja way of handling this. I might even go so far as to spill a glass of water by "mistake," or, better yet, suggest something requiring a physical response, such as: "Can everyone please check their water glasses right now? I found chips on some of them and I don't want you to cut your mouths." You get a half credit if you answered E. Ignoring a fart is never a bad idea; it's just that creating a diversion is more nunchi-ful. More like something Mrs. Ramsay would do.

CHAPTER 8

Nunchi at Work

DAVID BRENT: *The reason women wear necklaces is to draw attention to the breasts.*

WOMAN: *No ... I wear this because my mother gave it to me before she died.*

DAVID BRENT: *Well, she probably wore it to draw attention to hers.*

from the BBC television series The Office[10]

The David Brent character from the BBC series *The Office*, played by Ricky Gervais, is one of the best examples out there of the no-nunchi in the office. He thinks he's hilarious, and is blithely unaware of how uncomfortable people look when he tells jokes. He gives motivational speeches without realizing that no one feels motivated. When he gets £42,000 as part of a severance package, he spends it all on a professionally made music video of himself covering the 1980s ballad "If You Don't Know Me by Now" (with live doves), because he's horribly misjudged his star appeal.

A variation of the David Brent type is the office pest: the American sketch comedy show *Saturday Night Live* had a famous recurring skit with such a character, a low-level accountant called Richard, who wears a wrinkled shirt and sits right near the office photocopier. Every time someone comes to use the copier, he makes unnecessary small talk about photocopying: "Making copieeeeeees! Randy! The Rand-ster! Only one copy for the Rand-man!"

But for every work colleague with no nunchi, there is at least one with outstanding nunchi, who advances much further than their abilities indicate they could or should. It's that person who is reasonably competent but not overly so, yet constantly promoted for unclear reasons. And no, it's not because they're well connected or have slept with the right people. They simply have quick nunchi. To learn from such people, watch them watching others. They're always "eye-measuring."

Nunchi is crucial in the workplace because people will seldom tell you exactly what is happening. Owing to the fear of lawsuits and shareholder panic, companies will rarely be transparent about important information that affects you intimately, such as mass redundancies. It's up to you and your nunchi to work it out so you can ally yourself with the right people, distance yourself from the wrong people, or simply look for a job before the guillotine drops and you're all out on the job market competing for the same jobs at the same time.

I once worked at an office where it was announced that there would be an undisclosed number of redundancies. Everyone was speculating as to who would lose their jobs. It seemed clear to me that the three employees who had recently volunteered to be the office fire marshals would get sacked. And sure enough, they were all fired within a few months.

Was I psychic? Of course not. But I do have quick nunchi. Even so, why hone in on those three? They were all nice enough to volunteer to help with an orderly evacuation in the event of a fire. They liked people. Maybe a little too much, as they were more into socializing than they were into getting work done. They had misread the values of the office and focused on popularity rather than the work. My nunchi led me to believe that they had tried to compensate for this by volunteering for fire marshal.

The office had to find three more volunteers to fill those spots. I declined. Within a few months, two of the new fire marshals were sacked. Now I'm not saying that you shouldn't volunteer to help your colleagues, but if all the office underperformers gravitate to one activity (party committee, for example), maybe avoid that activity. At work, you are judged by the company you keep.

With quick nunchi, you can perform better at your job, enjoy it more, keep it longer, and get the pay raises you deserve.

Nunchi and the Titans of Business

Everyone in the pantheon of true business legends had massively quick nunchi. In no way does this mean that they were tactful at board meetings, nor does it mean they won popularity contests. You can be unpleasant and have quick nunchi, just as you can be kind and have bad nunchi. Nunchi is morally neutral; likeability is unrelated to nunchi levels.

The late Steve Jobs was famous for abruptness and his undisguised disdain for certain people, but everything points to his having had nunchi in spades. His greatest business triumphs occurred because he understood people better than people understood themselves.

In person, Jobs exercised the literal "eye" part of the eye-measure: he was famous for his penetrative stare.

Jobs also demonstrated tremendous nunchi when he predicted just how big a business digital music would become. He told author Walter Isaacson—who wrote Steve Jobs's authorized biography—that when Apple was first marketing the iPod, the company "outspent everybody by a factor of about a hundred."[11] Jobs was the pioneer of user-oriented design, and had an inflexible rule for the iPod developers that a user should be able to find any song within three clicks or fewer; he knew intuitively what users would find annoying. That's pure nunchi.

Another nunchi-ful tech titan was Bill Gates. In 2001, when he pushed into the video-game market with the release of the Xbox, Gates predicted that video games would soon be bigger business than movies. I remember thinking at the time that only a truly solipsistic game fanatic could possibly think that gaming was going to be that huge. But that shows what I knew: by 2004, Gates's prediction had already come true. Thanks to games such as *Halo* and *Call of Duty*, video games soon began to take a bigger market share than feature films. By 2018, annual video-gaming revenue had exceeded the combined revenue of movies *and* digital music.[12] This kind of foresight does not just come from Gates being a tech prodigy: it comes from his ability to eye-measure the public and to use his nunchi to sense which way the wind is blowing.

Jeff Bezos is another tech titan with lightning-quick nunchi: Amazon did not turn a profit for the first *fourteen years* of its existence, because Bezos insisted that the most important goal was to build a loyal customer base, and that profit would come later. Many thought he was crazy. But he understood the mind of the consumer in a way that only a nunchi master can. His steadfast vision was to create the world's first fully customer-centric company. His method proved so successful that other merchants followed suit with generous return policies. Now, he's created a market where it's becoming impractical for a consumer *not* to become an Amazon Prime member. The market value of Amazon's outstanding shares hit $1 trillion in 2018.

Jobs, Gates, and Bezos are excellent examples of the importance of Nunchi Rule #8: Be nimble, be quick. Their adaptability to changing market needs is central to their success.

The director Steven Spielberg (who brought us *Jaws*, *Indiana Jones*, *Schindler's List*, and much more) is as gifted at nunchi as he is at storytelling. In a widely covered and reprinted 1984 memo, an executive from the movie studio that was making the Spielberg-produced, iconic film *Back to the Future* expressed displeasure with the title. The exec's suggestion? *Spaceman from Pluto*.

Spielberg disagreed, but he didn't fire off a letter saying, "You just handle the money, OK?" In a 2015 interview with the pop culture site *ShortList*, *Back to the Future* screenwriter Bob Gale claimed that Spielberg replied with finesse: "Steven told us, 'Don't worry, I know how to handle him,' before writing a letter back which said, 'Hi Sid, thanks for your most humorous memo, we all got a big laugh out of it, keep 'em coming.' Steven knew [Sid] would be too embarrassed to say that he wanted us to take the letter seriously. Luckily nobody questioned the title after that. Without Steven, it could have all been very different."[13]

I'm sure you *think* you know counterexamples where nunchi is not synonymous with success: "But my boss is a David Brent clone, and yet he somehow got to the rank of CEO of an international corporation!" First, though, are you sure you're not confusing no-nunchi folk with people who are intentionally oblivious to other people? These two are not quite the same thing. A powerful business executive can have good nunchi and be rude to certain people by choice, just as one can be born with a naturally fast metabolism yet still become obese through poor eating choices.

Of course, there are many nunchi-deficient people in power, but for how long? And who knows how much further they would have got with better nunchi? It's likely that an executive with poor nunchi will run into some irreversible scandal or difficulty at some point. Sometimes this happens when people think they are so important that they don't need nunchi, and their colleagues are afraid to tell them the truth. That's when they crash and burn in a spectacular way.

This appears to have happened with Elon Musk, the technology entrepreneur, engineer, and cofounder of the all-electric vehicle company Tesla. He will never live down a series of poorly thought-out tweets from 2018, including one in which he used the word "pedo" to describe a diver who had rescued Thai schoolchildren trapped in a cave. To call those tweets a nunchi deficiency is an understatement.

In August 2018, Musk tweeted, "Am thinking of taking Tesla private at $420. Funding secured." First of all, this is not how you make a huge corporate announcement, before even clearing it with your own board or with the U.S. Securities and Exchange Commission. Second, he later explained that the $420 figure was a reference to the fact that 420 was slang for cannabis. This was further proof that Musk's nunchi had taken a holiday. If he thought that tweet would make him seem hip, this was a failure to read the room; he was brutally mocked in the media and on social media, where the line "Funding secured" became a joke meme.

In September of that year, the Securities and Exchange Commission charged Elon Musk with securities fraud and fined him $20 million. According to the SEC's official press release, the fraud was "for a series of false and misleading tweets about a potential transaction to take Tesla private."[14] Musk stepped down as chairman of Tesla that year.

Everyone makes mistakes. The hallmark of a nunchi-deficient person is that when they are wrong, they double down. This is what Musk did. In October 2018, after his disgrace, he tweeted that it had been "worth it"—not plausible and legally ill-advised, since the investigation was still ongoing at that point.

I'm not too worried for him, but it goes to show you that even though someone lacking in nunchi can get far in life, if you play stupid games, you will win stupid prizes.

What's the Political Landscape of Your Office?

Anyone with good nunchi understands that the office is not a trust-based environment. It is the epicenter of double-speak and passive-aggressive communication. Even if you love your colleagues, and think your boss is a genius, you would do well to keep your nunchi switched on at all times.

The good news is that if you're like most working stiffs, your nunchi at work is better than your nunchi in other areas of life because you're already on your guard. For example, I'd bet you have exercised quick nunchi in situations such as the following:

- A colleague who usually dresses in hoodies and yoga tights suddenly starts wearing a fancy suit to "doctor's appointments," and you realize this person is likely interviewing for a job. The following week, that colleague gives her notice.

- You notice that your colleague Ollie has started to be left out of meeting invites. At one meeting you play dumb and say, "Hey, should I go get Ollie?" and your boss says, "Nah, we can fill him in later." You then realize that the company is laying the groundwork for firing Ollie. A month later, that is precisely what happens.

You can probably think of dozens more examples of instances when nunchi saved your hide, or when a *lack* of nunchi cost you a pay raise, allies, or even a job.

With good nunchi, you can bring colleagues on board with an idea, without their even knowing you're doing it.

Imagine, for example, that you are part of a giant project that involves updating old payroll records. Most of your team think they should do the work themselves, in-house. But Darren thinks the work should be outsourced to another company. You and others are concerned that outsourcing the task will make your company outsource even more tasks, until none of you have a job. Darren says that he is too busy to update the records.

You need to resolve this quickly. Never let a debate go

on so long that it exhausts everyone. Usually, your bosses will get exasperated and make the decision for you. Plus, at the end of the day you still have to get along with your colleagues, and you don't want to win this battle at the expense of making it that much harder to persuade them in the future.

So what do you do? The good news is that colleagues will always (intentionally or not) tell you what you need to do to persuade them.

First, ask Darren why he thinks the project should be outsourced—even if you think you know what his answer will be. Pay attention to what he *doesn't* say.

He might say, "Too much work to do it in-house—simple as that." But why is he *not* addressing the real risk that outsourcing a big project could put him out of a job? Is it because he knows something you don't? Look at him: does he look smug? Maybe he knows his own job is secure because he's being handpicked for promotion, and he has no concern for what happens to the rest of you. Or is he behaving in an indifferent and lethargic way about other things? Maybe he plans to leave the company and just doesn't care about anything. Think about his behavior recently: have there been any signs he's been looking for a job? Either way, he's not on the same page as you. He's thinking short-term.

If you suspect this is the case, appeal to that. Put down your sword and drop your "but we'll get fired" whining. Offer to do Darren's portion of the payroll project for him—seriously—to get him to agree with you. Can you really manage the workload of two people? Probably not, but it doesn't matter. You've won. Not only have you eliminated Darren's only objection, but you've also impressed your colleagues and bosses that you're committed to this project and you intend to make their lives easier for them.

If this task is a top priority for the company, you can ask for extra resources or manpower *later*. They might even force Darren to do it after all; at that point, he can't refuse. In the short term, get their agreement, and create harmony. After that, all else becomes possible.

Being good at workplace nunchi means understanding what is being said between the lines, rather than in the official corporate announcement. Sure, it sounds charming when someone leaves the company to "pursue new opportunities" or "spend more time with their family," but most of us know that is simply an approved way of saying they got fired. What else isn't being said in your work environment?

Here are some examples of what people won't spell out for you, but which your nunchi might discern in a typical office setting:

- **Basic nunchi:** A group of people always look at each other when one of them makes a joke ➜ They're a clique.
- **Intermediate nunchi:** Someone is suddenly calling lots more meetings than before, on topics they could have covered in an email ➜ They've recently been in trouble with their boss.
- **Ninja nunchi:** A low-level employee is colossally stupid but never seems to get in trouble. Even the higher-ups are polite to them ➜ This person is being protected by someone powerful within the organization. Be nice.

Who is the best at getting other colleagues on board with their ideas, and how do they do it? Studying your work culture will give you the answers to the questions you didn't even know you should be asking.

What is prized in your workplace? Do you work in an office where everyone is at their desks by 8 a.m. or else? Or is your office a place where no one cares what time you arrive as long as you're coming up with creative ideas? Nunchi means reading the room, and understanding that every room, and every workplace, is different.

In France, I worked in an office where there was a lot of yelling. They thought that if I responded calmly, it meant

I wasn't taking them seriously. This was a culture shock to me, as my *anglo-saxon* side (as the French call it) advocates calmness in all situations and believes that the first person to raise their voice loses the argument. So, in order to get along with my French coworkers, I had to become a yeller as well. When, years later, I switched to an American office, I had to learn to stop yelling, or that would have been the end of my career.

And even within one company, work cultures change over time, sometimes incredibly fast. A change in management, for example, will fundamentally transform the work culture. If your old CEO had motivational posters saying things like "Teamwork" whereas your new CEO only has pictures of their sailboat, you are in a completely new office even if the company name in the lobby remains the same. The ability to read the room, even as it's changing, will always keep you nimble and adaptable.

Nunchi at a Work Meeting

If you are running the meeting, always—always—ALWAYS offer bite-size treats at the beginning. It needn't be lunch or anything fancy; even passing around a box of cheap mini chocolate bars is fine. Say (but don't yell), "Hi there, everyone, I brought [food item]." Make sure you use the word "everyone," which sets the tone that, at least for the one hour that you're in that conference room, you are all one organism.

Pass the snack to the person on your left, and tell everyone to "take one and pass it around." Don't leave the food in the middle of the table and tell everyone to "help themselves." That defeats the purpose. It's that circular motion of passing the treats that creates literal roundness. It ignites flow and connection in the room, like a relay race or passing the baton. It's a way of making people pay attention to others—at least the people to their left and right—which creates awareness of the "hive mind." This is effective even if people don't take the food. Furthermore, it creates an activity so that people get slightly less annoyed with their colleagues who are a few minutes late.

This energy circle you have created is a powerful unifying force that will make everyone cooperate better with one another, be more interested in what you and everyone else have to say, and increase the chance that you attain whatever your goal was in having that meeting.

And the exercise isn't just for them—it's for you, too! If they're eating, they're not talking. Even if their silence only lasts a few seconds, use that precious time to center yourself and take a few deep breaths, and don't forget to observe your colleagues.

Food eventually leads to chitchat. Good. You will learn from the ensuing conversation that Helen has ten dogs who love this brand of sweet, that Siobhàn's favorite flavor is cherry, that Julie has been dieting her whole life, and that David is half Belgian. For the ordinary person, these are throwaway comments. For the nunchi ninja, there is no such thing as a throwaway comment: it is all valuable data whether you need it now or not.

You will also discern where your colleagues' heads are at that moment: use those moments to see who looks tired, who looks irritated, who is frantically typing, who never takes your treats when they are annoyed at you. Use this data to adapt the meeting accordingly, and curry favor with those who clearly need it. If someone looks distracted, you should call on that person to give their opinion first to bring them back into the meeting. *Your* meeting.

If nothing else, feeding your guests is always good manners, and remember Nunchi Rule #5: Manners exist for a reason. Sometimes, it's a sort of Machiavellian one, such as gaining control of a meeting.

If you're not expected to participate in a meeting, take advantage of this golden opportunity to engage your nunchi and observe. Even if you hate meetings, start going to the ones that are "optional" (schedule permitting). You will learn ten times more about your colleagues in that meeting than at ones in which you are the center of attention.

Whose ideas always get emphatic nods of assent from the others? Whose ideas always seem to get shut down? Are there two people who always disagree, no matter what? If someone always manages to get people on his or her side by the end of the meeting, how does he or she do that? Do those whose voices get heard have better posture than the rest? Slower diction? Or are they putting nunchi in action— responding to any negative body language in the room by asking encouragingly, "I'd love to hear what you think"?

Noting these sorts of details will teach you more about office politics than if you were to interrogate every member of your team personally about their opinions on everything in the office.

Observe, observe, observe; listen, listen, listen. Two eyes, two ears, one mouth.

Nunchi and Office Socializing

Try this the next time your office has an outing or a drinks gathering. Upon entering the room, stand near the door before talking to anyone and take in the room as a whole, as if you had to paint it from memory later. Who is there, and where are they standing? Does their behavior make sense based on what you know about them? Does their body language signal a hierarchy that is different from what the organizational chart would suggest? Who is hovering by the food? The drinks? The boss?

You can learn a lot more about an office environment by reading the room than by reading the company's mission statement online.

Requesting a Pay Raise

Thea met with her boss, Ms. Chattypants, to ask for a salary increase. Thea had been offered a promotion already, but her new salary had not yet been decided.

As any good negotiator will tell you, you should try to find out the range the other person has in mind *before* you start talking numbers. And that means following Nunchi Rule #4: Never pass up a good opportunity to shut up. If you keep listening, the other party will tell you everything you need to know before you even ask.

Thea knew from previous observation that Chattypants had verbal diarrhea. If there was silence, Chattypants would feel obligated to fill it with the sound of her own voice. So Thea sat down with her and said simply, "I'd like to discuss a pay raise to accompany my recent promotion."

Then she left a silence that Chattypants felt obliged to fill. She told Thea, "I'm guessing you're cheesed off that we didn't give you the 3 percent cost-of-living increase last year."

Thea actually had no idea what Chattypants was on about, but remained *silent*. Which of course made Chattypants talk even more.

The latter continued, "OK, that's understandable." (Again, Thea had not said anything; she was not even aware she had been due a cost-of-living increase.) "Two years' worth of cost-of-living increases would be a 6 percent bump, but beyond that?"

Thea continued to say nothing. Chattypants continued, "I mean, I'm not going to pay you six figures or anything like that; that's 25 percent higher than the highest-ranking member of your team."

DING DING DING! That was the answer Thea was looking for. Without even realizing it, Chattypants had given her the exact range of what she should be asking for. Lower limit: a 6 percent increase on her current salary. Upper limit: $80,000, aka Thea's estimated salary of the highest-ranking member of her team, based on the data that Chattypants had blurted out ("six figures" being taken to mean $100,000). She knew that the company would come up with a lower but probably acceptable counteroffer, which they did. She ended up getting a 20 percent pay raise, and because Chattypants had shown her hand, Thea had the great satisfaction of knowing that she had not short-changed herself.

It is said that a fair negotiation does not start until at least one party is offended by the other's offer. If your boss is shocked by your number, do not cower. It means you did the right thing.

Hiring New Employees

There are steaming piles of manure who manage to shape-shift into humans during daylight hours and put on suits, and at least five of those people tend to get hired by whatever office I'm working in at the time. Your office as well, I'd wager. If those employees were there before you got there, that's one thing. But if you're fortunate enough to be in a position to interview job candidates before they're hired, summon 100 percent of your nunchi not only to screen the candidates, but to persuade your colleagues as to whom to hire. These shape-shifters always bring their friends to come to work with them, so even one of them is too many. They're also strangely difficult to fire.

People lie on their job applications more than ever, which means that if you're a hiring manager your nunchi has to be on high alert. Part of the problem is that the first round of résumé-reading is often performed by computer algorithms. If a candidate's application contains the magic keywords HR set for the job (for example, JavaScript, telemarketing, management), the algorithm will forward them to

HR. Otherwise, the candidate will receive an auto-reply rejection. Thus, candidates have taken to stuffing their applications with skills they don't have for fear of getting kicked out by a computer. This has unfortunately created a free-for-all on lying on *all* aspects of their experience.

Bad hiring managers treat the written application as a mere formality. "I have a good feeling about this candidate," they'll say, or "He had a nice, firm handshake" and that's all there is to it. But true nunchi doesn't mean that you *only* study body language and look into the person's eyes. It also means read—literally *read*—between the lines of the written résumé. That document allows you to connect the dots to the person sitting in front of you. If the dots don't connect, then you should set aside your "good feeling." And don't rule out the reality that "good feelings" and "bad feelings" about candidates might be the result of unconscious biases based on gender, race, hotness, and other factors that no one wants to admit they think about.

In my own office experiences, I have frequently been shot down when I tried to dismiss a candidate based on a dishonest application. "That's not a big deal," people will object if they found the person charming. But a hiring manager with quick nunchi knows that certain small gestures are *indicative* of much larger issues. Unfortunately, social pressure makes people feel petty about saying that anything is "indicative" of anything. I find, for example, that people who say that they are "fluent" in a language when they are not always end up being con artists of the first order.

Do not excuse the person by saying, "Well, the word 'fluent' is subjective." Are you kidding? It's not subjective at all. Some people claim fluency when they mean that they can order lunch in a restaurant. In fact, I see it as a kind of cultural insensitivity: lying about being fluent in any living language is an insult to the millions of people who actually speak it. Have the decency to say "working proficiency of..." or "beginning to learn..." No one will hate you for it.

People who habitually lie about their skills are bad news, whether the job requires those specific skills or not. This is the sort of person who coasts on not getting called out; they will never admit to not knowing something, even if colleagues would be more than happy to help. Rather, they bully the clever kids into doing their homework for them. Woe to you if you are that clever kid.

Nunchi and Stupid Colleagues

The astonishing thing about stupid people is the amount of influence they can wield in an office. This is due to the sheer stubbornness of their convictions, and the mysteries of how quickly bad ideas spread.

The truth is, if someone is really stupid, they're too stupid to know how stupid they are. The Dunning-Kruger effect is one of the most powerful forces in the universe, right up there with gravity and compound interest.

So how on earth do you contend with such a seemingly indomitable foe as nincompoopery? Reminding people that you think they're stupid is surprisingly ineffective; trust me, I've tried. Remember that your goal is never to prove that you're clever. It's to get them to agree with you so that you all don't get into trouble. Office nunchi means you need to think survival, not ego.

The really skilled nunchi practitioner uses the Socratic method. The ancient Greek philosopher Socrates was famous for playing dumb when trying to get people to agree with him. He asked questions of the other person to show them the logical extension of their argument. Socrates made the other person believe that whatever realization they came to was their own idea.

You have to be like Socrates. Why? Because everyone, no matter how clever or stupid, likes to believe that they have agency.

Here's an example of how this could go.

STUPID COLLEAGUE: OK, we need cute mouse images for our email blasts to the customers, but

Roberta from the art department is out sick, so I decided to copy and paste these Mickey Mouse images.

YOU: Oh, OK, so I take it you got permission from Disney, then? Amazing! How'd they get back to you so quickly?

STUPID COLLEAGUE: No, I didn't get permission. I'm sure it's fine.

YOU: Oh, OK, did our legal department finally get off our backs about *getting sued*? Gosh, they're so uptight, am I right?

STUPID COLLEAGUE: (*pauses*) Well, no, I didn't run this by legal. You know what? I just thought of another idea for where I can find images of cute mice. Disney is too much of a cliché.

So you see what's happened here? Stupid Colleague realizes you're probably right, but in using the Socratic method, you've given Stupid Colleague permission to pretend that it was his/her own idea to scrap the illegal use of copyrighted Disney images. You have allowed Stupid Colleague to save face. Stupid Colleague will be grateful for this.

Nunchi is basically mental martial arts: if someone attacks you with a galactically bad idea that will get everyone fired, don't exhaust yourself fighting them; instead, use the weight of their stubbornness against them. Flow with their stupidity and they might let go of it on their own.

Getting What You Want at Work

The most nunchi-ful way to get what you want at work is counterintuitive: work out what your boss wants and what *their* boss wants. Then find a way to present what *you* want as the solution to the problem: you'll get bonus points for solving a problem they didn't even know they had. The employee with great nunchi is always looking at more than just their individual role and their personal ambitions. They consider the company as a whole, and how their own goals fit in with the bigger picture, and they use that to their advantage.

Antony wants a promotion, but he knows the company he works for is going through a hard time financially. Although his work is excellent, and he feels ready for a managerial position, he is aware that going into his boss's office and asking flat out for a promotion may come across as tone-deaf in the current circumstances. Instead of feeling resentful at being held back, or whining with his colleagues about the lack of opportunities, Antony observes what is going on at work, with thoughts of his own promotion in mind. He notices that his boss seems particularly stressed out whenever she has catch-up meetings with her direct reports, of which there are many, including Antony. He overhears his boss grumbling to her own boss that managing the team is taking up time that she could be using to bring in new business.

At his next catch-up, Antony proposes a new team structure in which five of his boss's direct reports now report to him, taking a weight off her shoulders. It takes a few weeks of discussions, but the team is restructured as he proposed, and he gets his promotion. Crucially, his boss now considers him a smart and ambitious problem solver instead of a person complaining about not getting promoted.

Take time to observe your boss, and to analyze what their main priorities are, and work out how you can make the most of the opportunities these present to you, as the nunchi-ful employee.

Interviewing for a New Job

"So, let's start with the elephant in the room," a job recruiter once said to me within minutes of my sitting down across from her desk.

I was interviewing for a job at a magazine. I had no idea what she was on about with this elephant business. My nunchi told me to be silent, even though I was thinking, "Did she hear something bad about me? Do I have poppy seeds in my teeth?"

She continued, "The recent round of redundancies we had were *not* due to financial problems. The magazine was rebranding, redoing our image, and some of our old-guard employees were not supportive of that. It's not as if we push our senior staff out on an ice floe."

All I needed to know for that interview rained down upon me in the first three minutes of being in that room, before I'd even said anything about myself. What could one deduce from only these few sentences? That they had fired not one but many high-ranking and probably highly paid employees, and that they had developed such a bad reputation for this that HR had to apologize for it pre-emptively. So, maybe not the best place to work. I also knew that supposing I did want to impress the hiring manager in the next round of interviews, I would need to emphasize how adaptable I was to corporate rebrandings and how much I loved the magazine's new image.

I was not called back. I don't know whether they filled the job. All I know is that less than a year later, a different HR recruiter from the same company contacted me on LinkedIn about the exact same job. In other words, the company was having trouble retaining not only the person they had hired, but also its HR recruiters. This would not have been hard to predict, based on the first few minutes of that initial HR interview.

At any interview, let the other person speak as much as possible and resist the urge to interrupt and tell them how great you'd be at the job. Why? Because the interviewer will give away their hand and tell you exactly what they are looking for, what the company values are, and maybe even why they got rid of the person you'd be replacing. If you know that, you can confidently say the right thing.

Your nunchi's biggest source of power? The fact that people talk too much.

A lot of job seekers get annoyed with sometimes having to be screened by the HR recruiter rather than being sent straight to the hiring manager, but are they kidding? A first-round HR interview is a gift from the heavens. Recruiters are there to sell the company to you, so they will talk a great deal. Your job is to let the recruiter talk until they can talk no more. This will tell you more about how to speak to the hiring manager than the hiring manager could ever tell you him- or herself.

No matter how rosy a picture the recruiter paints, if you read between the lines you can get a strong sense of the good, the bad, and the ugly. They're practically feeding you the script of what to say for the rest of your interview.

It harks back to Nunchi Rule #4: Never pass up a good opportunity to shut up. If you wait long enough, most of your questions will be answered without your having to say a word.

The First Week at a New Job

Remember Nunchi Rule #3: If you just arrived in the room (in this case, a new job), remember that everyone else has been there longer than you. Watch them to gain information. Please don't try to make a splash, be witty, or buy everyone sushi in your first few days. Those gestures don't go nearly as far as people seem to think. You *should* introduce yourself to everyone you run into, mainly for the purpose of feeling them out, not for immediately seeking allies and gossip. You should prioritize being observant over being charming.

Don't reveal anything personal if you can avoid it, even if it seems harmless, such as where you live or how many kids you have. The moment you talk about yourself, you're shutting down your nunchi because you're forgetting to pay attention.

Remember, at a new job, optics are everything in those first few months. Heed the old saying "He who has a reputation as an early riser may sleep until noon." In other words, if you establish your image early on as a diligent and reliable worker, people will cut you a great deal of slack later.

Nunchi for Those Who Hate Their Jobs

I hear you. You might be in a job situation so irremediable that none of my advice so far resonates. You might have a pervert colleague, a sadistic boss, or an inhumane sick-leave policy. And depending on your field, the state of the economy or whom you are supporting at home, you might not be able to get your head around finding another job at the moment.

If this is the case, I offer up this quotation from the Korean Buddhist monk Haemin Sunim, author of the international bestseller *The Things You Can See Only When You Slow Down*:

> When you leave work for the day, if you find yourself asking, "Do I have to live my whole life like this?" then try the following: Wake up a little earlier the next morning, and sit in silence, as if in meditation. Breathe in deeply and slowly, and ask yourself how your work is helping others, regardless of how insignificantly or indirectly. As you focus on others, you can reconnect with the meaning and purpose of your work.

That's nunchi at its noblest, so I'll repeat it: Ask yourself *how your work is helping others, regardless of how insignifi-*

cantly or indirectly. Maybe you get to help customers once in a while. Maybe you're expected to work such late hours that you're there when the cleaning staff arrive. But maybe you're also the only person who says hello to those cleaners, and don't they really deserve to be acknowledged? Why not make them coffee or offer them one of your biscuits? They'd rather be at home too; it's not all about you.

Will these gestures make you walk to an odious job with a spring in your step? Probably not, but it will give you something even more important: a sense of meaning in the midst of pointless drudgery.

QUICK QUIZ

Answer these questions about your office. Don't think, just answer. There are no right answers; this is your own nunchi exercise.

A. In one sentence, describe what personality traits your workplace seems to value the most.

B. Explain how you arrived at your answer for question A.

C. In your current or past workplaces, who was a morning person and who was decidedly not a morning person?

D. Have you experienced a double standard in how people are treated when they have personal appointments? For example, does person X seem to go to their kids' school plays with no one batting an eyelid, whereas person Y always seems to get in trouble for the exact same behavior? If so, why do you think they are treated differently?

E. Are the quiet people in your office getting more work done than the rest, or are they simply quiet? Do they seem to get more or less respect than their noisier peers?

If you didn't have ready answers, use the next work meeting as an opportunity to watch your colleagues. It doesn't matter whether you get to the bottom of all of these; the point is to switch on your nunchi and give your senses something to latch on to. You'll learn far more than the answers to just these particular questions.

CHAPTER 9

Nunchi for the Nervous

One reason I wrote this book is that many other advice books seem to offer "help" that I don't consider helpful. Often the advice is tantamount to "You have to already be OK to become OK." You know, like, "Love yourself or no one will love you." What is that, blackmail? Why not just tell everyone to kill themselves, already?

One of the best things about nunchi is that you don't have to be *at all* OK to benefit from using it. You can profit from it whether you're on top of the world or at your most abject, and everything in between. In fact, when you are at your most anxious, your nunchi is at its sharpest—remember, that it is the advantage of the underdog.

That said, you do have to *open your mind* to your nunchi—and activate the awareness that is there and ready to help you.

I'm saying this from painful life lessons that I have had to learn because I didn't heed my nunchi the first time.

I have been medically treated for social anxiety in the past, so I'm all too aware that it can be crippling for some people. Unfortunately, though, social anxiety is one of those ailments for which the only 100 percent effective remedy—removing yourself from humans—is not practical or sensible. Sometimes people fantasize that becoming very wealthy will allow them to avoid people, only to discover that success has exactly the opposite effect.

But if you feel this way, why would focusing on other people be helpful at all? Aren't they the problem?

Well, in some ways they are the problem, but to the nunchi ninja they are also the solution. Or, rather, shifting the way you view them is the solution.

To refer once more to the Stoics, you have to focus on what you can control, which is your own judgment and actions.

Everyone from your religious leader to your therapist will tell you that the best nonmedical remedy for depression is to help other people. Similar logic applies to social anxiety: the best nonmedical remedy is nunchi. You can use your powers of nunchi to focus your energy away from your own discomfort and on to those around you.

Buddhists refer to anxieties as the "monkey mind." Think

of your anxiety as a twitchy, loud monkey that you can't get rid of because it is part of who you are. If you fight the monkey or chain it up, it will only get even angrier and louder. What you can do, however, is throw it a distracting object while shouting, "Go get it, boy! Atta boy! Good monkey." Maybe don't say that last part out loud if you're on a podium and about to address the United Nations or something, but you get the idea.

Buddhists say you can keep the monkey busy by telling it to focus on your breathing. So when you feel social anxiety coming on, breathe deeply and calmly, and remember that, for the next few minutes, you are an observer. "We're just here to watch, Monkey."

If you are anxious while talking to people, remember Nunchi Rule #1 and empty your mind: don't think about what impression you might be making. Instead, study your counterparts as if you were being paid to file a detailed Sherlock Holmes-type report on them later. Mentally note details: are they out of breath? If so, they could have asthma, or maybe they're out of shape. Or perhaps they are as nervous or anxious as you are! A vomit stain on the shoulder? A baby at home, perhaps. Paint a mental picture with those details: how would a woman like that dress her baby? Is the baby's room pink, blue, or gender-neutral? You're world-building and your conclusions might be inaccurate, but it honestly doesn't matter. Right now you're trying to take the focus off yourself and reduce anxiety that way. If you still find their humanness oppressive, then stop focusing on them as individuals. Remind yourself that the unit of nunchi is the room—step outside of yourself and take in the room as a whole tableau, like one of those giant wall-sized paintings of coronations or picnics that you see in museums.

I know that if you are on the verge of a panic attack at the thought of an upcoming, high-stakes social situation, advice such as "silence your mind" or "focus on others" might make you answer sarcastically, "Wow, thanks, I'm cured." Fair enough. But believe me when I tell you that nunchi can get you through some of the most challenging life experiences, primarily by taking your focus off yourself.

Instead of being anxious about banal small talk, how about *not* making banal small talk? How about listening to others talk for a bit? If you watch and listen attentively— i.e., *use your goddamned nunchi*—people will give you more than enough information for you to know what to say next.

Note: social anxiety is different from simply hating people, which I'm afraid nunchi can't really help you with.

Adaptability

I mentioned earlier that I was not born with naturally quick nunchi. I acquired it because I had to adapt to major life changes, starting with my family's move from the U.S. to Korea when I was twelve. I am a nunchi late bloomer, and am constantly humbled by how much I have yet to learn.

Everyone has to start their life over several times; I am no exception. My international moves never really stopped, taking me to Frankfurt, Berlin, Paris, New York—and I lived in some of those cities more than once.

I'm not saying these moves make me better or even wiser than anyone else. What I am saying is that the experience has made me more adaptable. So I think I'm on pretty firm ground here when I assure you that while I think it's total bullshit that "what doesn't kill you makes you stronger," it is absolutely the case that your *observation and adaptability* will make you stronger.

Moving from country to country alerts you to the differences between cultures in ways that can be quite jarring. A gesture that is innocuous in the United States might be considered obscene in Italy. The unspoken rules of the road in Europe are entirely different in Asia. But there are also smaller cultural shifts within one country, and even within one city. Being able to observe and adapt will serve you wherever you go.

Anxiety versus Nunchi

"Trusting your gut" isn't always as clear-cut as it seems. If you are on a date with someone you really like, for example, you might not be sure which of your thoughts are coming from your gut, which are from your mind, which are from your heart, and which are from your nether regions. You'll sometimes be confused about your nunchi as well. For example, if your blood suddenly runs cold, is it because of an irrational anxiety, such as a phobia that ducks will come to your home to murder you, or is it your nunchi alerting you to real danger?

I believe that to some degree bad nunchi isn't really bad nunchi; it's people not willing to connect the dots between their nunchi and their agency. At the point when it starts to dawn on people that collecting data has to result in making a decision, they muffle their nunchi like a hostage and put it in the trunk of their car. They are afraid of the truth. They don't want to think about the possibility that they are indeed an embarrassing drunk or that their very attractive companion is lying to them; they'd much rather distract themselves with more exciting nonexistent problems...like killer ducks.

If you're not sure whether your fears are irrational anxieties or your nunchi trying to get your attention, the first thing you should do is locate where that feeling is in the body.

When your nunchi has taken in and processed data, any resulting strong feelings such as fear will be felt most vividly in your gut. It will feel cold and factual, even if it feels terrible. If you are feeling anxiety, this is usually your smarty-pants cerebral cortex making you confused, and you will feel it in two places at once: the head, but mostly the chest. If it feels like an anvil is slowly crushing your chest and making it hard to breathe, that's anxiety, not nunchi.

Nunchi triggers your survival skills, your fight-or-flight response. These are the same skills that allow a mother to somehow sense her child is in trouble, allowing her to dash with lightning speed to the bedroom and giving her the preternatural strength to lift the heavy oak dresser that has fallen on her child. Anxiety allows you to do none of those things.

Connecting specific feelings to specific body parts takes some practice. I'd say you have to do this on around ten separate real-life occasions before it starts to feel natural. You have a significant advantage here if you practice yoga, meditation or any sport that requires mind–body awareness; for me, it's Pilates. If my Pilates instructor tells me, "You should be feeling this exercise more in the lats and less in the biceps," then I know how to mentally switch on the lats so that more power radiates from that area. This kind of reflex will quicken the rate at which you discern how your thoughts and feelings connect to specific bodily organs.

If you think that sounds New Age, think about your own experiences: if you have been trying to solve a thorny math problem for hours, it's your head that will hurt, not your big toe. If you walk in on the love of your life having sex with someone else, you will feel as if someone kicked you in the solar plexus, not your right ear. You are aware of connections between feelings and specific body parts all the time.

The Nunchi-ful Traveler

Nunchi ninjas are a delight to travel with. They can go to a pharmacy or grocery store in a country they've never been to before, and where they don't speak the language, and yet magically gravitate toward the correct aisle for the pomegranate juice or the snake-bite cream as if they'd been shopping there their whole lives. They can successfully get directions from someone without sharing the same language. They choose a great restaurant without consulting a guide, just going on their gut feelings.

These people are finely tuned to the differences between cultures but, more than that, they are delighted by them. They see the differences as something to embrace, as part of the experience of traveling in a new country. Their abilities come naturally to them, but all of us can work on developing our powers of observation in order to be a welcome guest in any country.

Meanwhile, the nunchi-deficient are exasperating, and the cause of many fights. One frequently hears of a couple breaking up after a big trip together—or, indeed, right in the middle of it. A huge reason for this is that one party's lack of nunchi was thrown into sharp focus in a foreign environment and the other party simply could not believe their eyes.

Nunchi-deficient travelers crap in the bidet. They accidentally insult the locals. They lose money in street gambling games or are overcharged at the market because they have no idea how much cheese should cost. They allow themselves to take the bait of being distracted and then pickpocketed. They go to dangerous neighborhoods because they can't pick up on the danger signs. They flip out because they can't cope with being lost. Sometimes they even endanger the safety of their traveling companions. That's when their nunchi deficiency goes from funny to mildly annoying to... "This person makes me feel unsafe. Is this someone I really want as a friend/life partner?"

Nunchi-deficient people don't travel well because they tend to be neurotically afraid of change. Not coincidentally, the inability to adapt to change is also a huge factor in breakups. Change is the essential skill of the nunchi master.

Though you are probably unlikely to be a full-on no-nunchi individual, even slight nunchi deficiencies will prevent you from enjoying traveling as much as you could, thereby depriving yourself of one of life's greatest joys and one of life's best nunchi-sharpening experiences.

The Rules for Correct Nunchi Travel Behavior

As my nunchi-ful friend Helen says, "One of the biggest mistakes in life is assuming that everyone is like you." It's true in life; it's true in travel.

Here are examples of requests that friends visiting me in Paris have wanted me to deal with:

- "Tell them I want the twelve-course tasting menu, but can they make all the dishes vegetarian?"
- "Tell them I want to speak to the manager about this slow service."
- (Outside on a restaurant terrace, with an ashtray on every table) "Tell that couple their smoking is triggering my allergies."

If you really cannot see yourself refraining from these kinds of tone-deaf requests, do the world a favor and stay at home playing video games or something. Let your passport expire; do not renew it.

Of course, it's impossible to be omniscient about a country you have never visited. Here are some universal guidelines that will help you on 90 percent of the earth's habitable surface:

Nunchi Abroad Rule #1:
Do as the Romans do

Professor Minsoo Kang, who grew up all over the world, owing to his father having been in the Korean diplomatic corps, is particularly adept at expat nunchi. He points out that in Iran, where he once lived, "You have to be careful about complimenting something or they will give it to you and get offended if you don't take it."

A nunchi-deficient traveler might refuse to believe these cultural traditions. But why would you think people were fabricating this kind of advice? Why would you then insist, "I understand what you're saying, but I've just got to be me?"

Let's say you then go to the home of an Iranian government official and admire a valuable lamp, and they give it to you. The good news is you have a nice lamp. The bad news is that you will never know whether the host really wanted to part with that lamp. They might never invite you back, and instead talk about you for evermore as that dreadful foreigner who, for all intents and purposes, burgled their home.

I admit to having violated this rule before (again, I was not born with quick nunchi; it was acquired through trial and error), for example refusing to wear a hijab in areas where I was advised to wear it for my own safety. I thought I was making an important feminist statement with my uncovered head; instead, I was wasting local resources because various hotel staff and police had to keep making sure I was OK and not being harassed.

Nunchi Abroad Rule #2:
No one is obligated to translate everything for you unless they have specifically been hired to do so

I've seen people get agitated when someone is speaking a language they don't know, because of some irrational fear that they are being talked about by every single person around them. Just stop. Sit with the discomfort of not understanding everything.

Nunchi Abroad Rule #3:
No one cares that you're entitled to service X because "That's how it's done where I am from"

This is tantamount to telling a date they should have sex with you because some other person had sex with them after being taken to the same restaurant.

If you're visiting a country where tipping is customary, don't say, "Sorry, we don't tip in my country." If you're visiting a country where restaurants charge you for bread and pretzels, the fact that you disagree with this practice is not the restaurant's problem.

Observe and adapt; do not ask an entire culture to adapt to you instead.

Nunchi Abroad Rule #4:
Learn how to say these three things in any language: a) "Hello"; b) "Can you help me?"; and c) if you don't speak the language, "Do you speak [my language]?"

I remember one American telling me, unprompted, "I visited Paris once; I hated it. I went to the customer window in the Métro to ask for help and they wouldn't help me. It's their job to help me!"

Upon enquiring further, I learned that he had immediately started barking questions in English to the Métro employee. Jesus wept. I could see why someone might not want to help this sort of person.

OK. First of all, unless you are on fire, when speaking to someone in a foreign country, always give a polite greeting *in the person's own language* before you say anything else. In France, you say "*Bonjour*," and you wait for them to say "*Bonjour*" back. Remember Nunchi Rule #5: Manners exist for a reason.

Saying "*Bonjour*," or whatever the greeting may be, is not some time-wasting relic from another century; it's how you signal to the person that you want to say something. You need to wait for their response, so they can snap out of where their mind was and give you their undivided attention. People from most nations require a mutual greeting before a conversation can take place, whether among friends or strangers.

Even if you're not sure what the local protocol is, please err on the side of caution and start any request for help with the equivalent of "Hello," even if it's just "Hello" in English (or any language). There is no culture on earth where people will laugh at you or hate you for saying hello before launching into a request.

Second, why would you ever begin speaking a language that is not the local tongue without any prior warning? Even people who speak multiple languages often get confused if someone suddenly switches languages on them. If you are planning to speak English or any other language that is not normally spoken in a given country, please always start by asking, "Do you speak [my language]?" This readies the other person mentally to switch to another language, or to find someone else who can help you.

Nunchi Abroad Rule #5:
If in doubt, try to read body language

This is what Minsoo Kang did while visiting a professor at Cambridge University. Kang was educated in the West and he speaks English perfectly, but even then, someone with quick nunchi never takes for granted that they understand everything just because they speak the local language. You need to pay attention to other clues. As the Irish playwright George Bernard Shaw wrote, "England and America are two countries divided by a common language."

Kang said, "The whole time I was talking to [the professor], I had a feeling that being in his office was an intrusion. He was very polite, but I could tell that he could not wait for me to get out. So I said, 'Thank you for your time' and got up to leave. He then asked if I wanted to go to his home for dinner with his family. I assumed he was only being polite, so I declined."

It turned out Kang's nunchi was accurate in picking up

the professor's mood. When Kang returned to the United States, the colleague who had arranged Kang's meeting with the Cambridge professor gave Kang some surprising information: "The professor thought you were great! Do you know why he thought you were great? Because you turned down his invitation to dinner."

Kang's conclusion was: "The fact that I declined means I did him a favor; in his mind now I'm someone who's very polite. In the English sensibility, that's polite."

Always Consider Context

When it comes to nunchi, you are often your worst enemy, especially if you are anxious about what others think. You sometimes quash your nunchi if you're worried it will tell you something you don't want to hear. For example, you may fear criticism. But you shouldn't fear it. I am not saying you should believe everything critical that people say of you, just don't be afraid of it. Your nunchi will tell you whose words are worth listening to. If someone is only trying to put you down rather than help you rise, your nunchi will tell you.

There is a nunchi paradox, which is that in order to stop worrying what people think of you, you have to concern yourself with what people think of you. That said, please disregard anything people say to you on social media. They can't eye-measure you and you can't eye-measure them, and you're both playing to a global audience, not just to each other. If a twelve-year-old were to insult you while playing video games in their mother's basement, would you take it seriously? No, you'd laugh. For all you know, that's what people tweeting at you are doing. Social media is a no-nunchi clusterfuck. There is no wisdom in those crowds.

Instead, take into account who is criticizing you and what their intention might be. You might assume your friend is telling you to interrupt people less because she's "just jealous," and maybe she is ... or maybe she's giving you great advice that no one else can give you because you keep cutting them off. A manager turning you down for a job because your experience is "too erratic" might just be a stick in the mud ... or maybe you get nervous in interviews and give the impression of instability. Prioritize face-to-face feedback and try not to become defensive straight away. Putting your defenses up immediately blocks your nunchi.

Nunchi and Depression

Sometimes you feel too broken to think about self-improvement. Anyone at a low point thinks, "I don't even care what happens to me or whether I wake up tomorrow morning, so how can I summon the energy for nunchi?"

But you know what? Your reptilian brain and your

survival instincts disagree with you. The reptilian brain wants to live. Even the most suicidal person will duck out of the way if someone tries to punch them in the face. Even the most dejected person sitting in their car, about to take a fistful of sleeping pills, is going to slam on the accelerator and drive away as fast as they can if a big brown bear were to start running toward them at full speed while growling. It's just instinct.

Or course, if there are particular individuals who always trigger anxiety because of a toxic dynamic between the two of you, then for the love of heaven get rid of them. As your body gets older and more tired, you'll need to preserve that energy for everything from staving off illness to looking after yourself and your loved ones. To quote a popular internet meme, "If you are depressed, first consider the possibility that you're just surrounded by assholes."

QUICK QUIZ

Which of these situations describe nunchi-based healthy fears, and which describe irrational anxiety?

YOUR CONCERN		NUNCHI OR ANXIETY? (CIRCLE ONE)
A.	You see your boyfriend being jumpy and evasive with his phone. You suspect he might be hiding something.	Nunchi / Anxiety
B.	You meet an attractive woman at your boyfriend's office and think, "My boyfriend is going to have an affair with that person," based solely on the woman's beauty and no other data.	Nunchi / Anxiety
C.	You see your teenage child suddenly start to display hair-trigger anger and notice money disappearing from your wallet. You suspect drugs.	Nunchi / Anxiety
D.	You notice your teenage child listening to ska music. You suspect drugs.	Nunchi / Anxiety
E.	Your boss has stopped including you in meetings and has asked you to train another employee in all your skills. You conclude you are getting fired.	Nunchi / Anxiety
F.	Your boss is slamming doors and screaming at you to hurry up with a project. You conclude you are getting fired.	Nunchi / Anxiety

Correct answers: A, C, and E are examples of nunchi-based observations. They are reactions to behavior that should lead you at the very least to ask some careful questions. Concerns B, D, and F are irrational anxieties, based on nothing more than the person's own prejudices or insecurities.

Whether you are anxious, depressed, or simply in a strange environment, remember the Korean saying "Nunchi is the secret weapon of the underdog." No matter how broken you are, nunchi can lift you up again. Don't think of nunchi as a difficult exercise or philosophy; think of it as a powerful inner strength that gets even stronger during emergencies. The capacity for nunchi is already in your genes, having persisted and evolved over millions of years for the sake of your well-being. Happiness and success are already in you...and outside of you. Being interested in the world outside yourself is the first step toward happiness and success. You've got this.

Conclusion

Nunchi is perhaps the most important skill you will ever learn—a skill that gets to the core of being human.

In Korea, nunchi is interwoven with life from childhood till death. In the West, the time to adopt nunchi principles has not only arrived, it is long overdue.

As Koreans say, half of public life is nunchi. And it's not a mystical Eastern concept. At heart, it's a Western one too; but many people have forgotten about the importance of paying attention to those around you because of the persistent and growing myth of self-reliance.

People like to think that they created communities entirely by their own choice, but they're kidding themselves. As Aristotle wrote, communities arose because we needed them to survive. When you accept that group life is a necessity, you understand that nunchi is a necessity.

Exercising nunchi can dissipate some of the anxiety you have about social interactions. The pressure is off, since you don't have to make people like you in order to get along with them or get what you want from them. Part of nunchi is accepting that we're all in this boat together, for good and for bad. And by boat, I don't just mean planet Earth or wherever the winds blow you, I mean the room that you are in at any given time. Wherever you are, you can use your nunchi.

Nunchi is a manifestation of the American expression "Work smarter, not harder." Of course, preparation and hard work are incredibly important. However, there is no substitute for nunchi—for observing quietly and adapting your behavior in real time.

If you have quick nunchi, you can create a harmonious environment, which makes people want to be around you. But that's only half the point of nunchi; it's not meant to be a popularity contest. The other half of nunchi is entirely pragmatic: it makes you successful at influencing people. Nunchi may sound Machiavellian, but in fact everyone wins. By creating a round, pleasant atmosphere, everyone benefits.

Nunchi is crucial to success and happiness. It can make you a better parent, partner, son or daughter, colleague, boss, and friend.

Don't get me wrong, some people can get pretty far in life with bad nunchi, but imagine how much further they'd have got if their nunchi were better. There are certainly highly visible, highly powerful people who seemingly have no nunchi, but in many cases this is their own choice; their hubris became such that they stopped paying attention to the evidence of their senses. Their egos suppressed their nunchi. They stopped listening to advisers, or perhaps those advisers gave up.

You can only get so far by being pushy. If you don't use your nunchi, your success will collapse in on itself. This is true of any great leader—or even a great empire.

Let's remind ourselves of the eight rules of nunchi:

1. First, empty your mind. Remember the words of Bruce Lee: "Empty your cup, so that it may be filled." Step back, breathe, and remember that prejudice prevents you from learning anything about other people.

2. Be aware of the Nunchi Observer Effect. When you enter a room, you change the room. Understand your influence. Your presence is already changing the environment without you saying a word. There's no need for a big opening act.

3. If you just arrived in the room, remember that everyone else has been there longer than you. Watch them to gain information. If everyone looks sad, don't try to cheer everyone up until you have more data. If everyone is seated in a circle on the floor

engaged in some activity, don't break up the activity unless it's clear they're summoning Satan.

4. Never pass up a good opportunity to shut up. If you wait long enough, most of your questions will be answered without you having to say a word. This advice will serve you well in negotiations, where the goal is to learn as much as possible while keeping your cards close to your chest.

5. Manners exist for a reason. Don't dismiss them as superficial; they're used to make people feel comfortable.

6. Read between the lines. People don't always say what they are thinking and that's their prerogative. If it makes someone anxious to be blunt, then don't put them in that position; pay attention to context and to what they are *not* saying.

7. If you cause harm unintentionally, it's sometimes as bad as if you'd caused it intentionally. Intent is not impact, as the saying goes. Intent is just based on what's in your own head; you need to get outside of your head to make people comfortable around you. Try to create roundness, not jagged edges.

8. Be nimble, be quick. Gather data quickly, process quickly, adapt quickly. The room you entered ten minutes ago is not the same room that you are in

now. Everything is in flux. Remember: survival of the fittest doesn't mean survival of the strongest. It means survival of the most adaptable.

When Nunchi Seems Too Hard

If you really, really can't be silent, all is not lost. There are other ways to read a room, such as looking directly into people's eyes. If people find it mildly intimidating, that can be the whole point. That's your leverage, right there. As mentioned, Steve Jobs was known for staring into people's eyes.

If you think carefully about people you know who are completely lacking in nunchi, they might be good, bad, or anything in between, but the one thing they have in common is that they do not appear to be in control of their own lives. In the worst-case scenario, they are letting dangerous people influence them. In the best-case scenario, they alienate people without knowing why, have trouble advancing at work, and lose friends as quickly as they make them.

Using nunchi doesn't mean losing yourself in the other person. Quite the opposite, in fact. If you are observing and discerning from a place of inner stillness, you are understanding the person as they truly are, from a safe and objective distance. Nunchi makes you brave—both in appearance and in reality.

Having quick nunchi will allow you to live your life deliberately. There will always be people who don't like you; that's inevitable. But at least don't make things harder for yourself by unintentionally making people hate you for entirely preventable reasons.

You will make nunchi errors now and then. Don't beat yourself up over it; even nunchi ninjas make faux pas. No one is perfect. And if you do put your foot in it? Don't fret. Let it go. The nunchi ninja knows that the steadfast rule is "Least said, soonest mended."

Most people in social situations try to say something clever. But cleverness is vastly overrated, and worrying over the smartest thing to say will distract you from observing others. What will get you much further in life is the ability to read the climate in the room. Developing your nunchi will unblock so many areas of your life. People will flock to your side without even knowing why.

If you think of yourself as always being in a wrestling match with the world, your nunchi will help you to release that grasp and make the world work with you.

That colleague who reflexively shoots down all your ideas will start to find fewer excuses to disagree with you. The clerk whose job it is to tell everyone "no" will say to you, "Well, I suppose there is a backdoor method we could try..." Questions you silently pose to yourself, such as, "What does a person have to do to get heard around here?" will answer themselves without your having to say a word. You will discover that tough negotiations seem more like a tango than a fight. You will be less anxious in social situations.

No matter what surprises await you in any room or situation, be confident that you have all the tools you need to create roundness, make people respond harmoniously to you and vice versa, and make the universe bend a little to your will. You don't have to be the best in order to win; all you need is your eyes and your ears.

Advanced Nunchi

By this point you probably have a good idea of how you can begin to use nunchi in your daily life. But the key is practice. I know several high financiers who play chess to sharpen their minds; similarly, Koreans have plenty of games that sharpen their nunchi. Here are two popular Korean games that require quick nunchi. One is called the Nunchi Game; the second is called *muk-ji-pa*. Both are purely social games, in that they don't use equipment, dice or game accoutrements of any kind.

The Nunchi Game

This is often played as a drinking game, but it's really difficult to win even if you are sober. Korean variety shows often make famous celebrities and K-pop stars play it.

Basically, it involves counting. One player (doesn't matter who; it's self-selecting) shouts the number "One!" while standing up, then quickly sits back down. After that, someone shouts "Two!" while standing up, then quickly sits back down. And so forth. If you are the last person to "claim" a number, you lose. If you repeat a number someone has just said, you are eliminated. If two people jump up and say the same number at the same time, they are both eliminated, even if it is the correct number. You play rounds of the game until one person is left standing; that remaining individual is the winner.

The game is 100 percent nunchi. To win, you must be quick and psych out your opponents. For example, if someone looks poised to jump, you can lean forward as if you are about to jump, thereby confusing your opponent into calling the wrong number.

Muk-ji-pa

Muk-ji-pa is a variation of the game known in the West as "rock-paper-scissors," with some major differences. Literally translated, *muk* means "rock," *ji* means "scissors" and *pa* means "paper." (Note that the order of the words for this particular game is different from the Western version: rock-scissors-paper, as opposed to rock-paper-scissors.)

The differences between rock-paper-scissors and muk-ji-pa

1. In rock-paper-scissors, both players are playing an offensive position, and have the same goal: they're trying to throw down the dominant hand gesture. Rock defeats scissors, scissors defeats paper, paper defeats rock. But in muk-ji-pa, by contrast, one player is in an offensive position and the other is in a defensive position, and neither player is trying to throw down the dominant hand gesture. Rather, you're either trying to throw down the same gesture as your opponent (if you are playing offense), or a different gesture from your opponent (if you are playing defense).

2. In rock-paper-scissors, two people throwing down the same hand gesture is considered a tie. In muk-ji-pa, two people throwing down the same hand gesture means a win for the offense and a loss for the defense.

3. In rock-paper-scissors, the game ends when one person's gesture is dominant over the other person's gesture; for example, if Player A plays paper and Player B plays scissors, B is the victor and the game is over. But in muk-ji-pa, a paper–scissors outcome

does not mean scissors wins; it only means that for the following round, A plays defense and B plays offense. The game is not over until both players play the same hand (e.g. both A and B play scissors).

4. Rock-paper-scissors usually ends quickly; for example if, in Round 1, one player throws rock and one throws paper, then paper wins and the game is over after just one round. By contrast, muk-ji-pa can go on for many rounds, before both throw down the same hand gesture.

5. To make matters more complicated, the person playing offense is required to shout out his/her hand (muk, ji, or pa), while the person playing defense is required to be silent.

6. Rock-paper-scissors is mostly a game of chance, whereas muk-ji-pa is mostly a game of nunchi.

The key to winning muk-ji-pa is anticipating which of the three objects your opponent is going to make.

Since both players are throwing these gestures simultaneously, you have to use your nunchi to guess what your opponent will do.

A player with quick nunchi can tell from your face, reactions, and body gestures what you are about to throw down. They may also notice you have certain patterns.

For example, it is well known that novices in muk-ji-pa are loath to use the same hand gesture twice in a row, and almost never use it three times in a row. An experienced player knows this and will use it to their advantage.

An inexperienced player will fix their attention on the opponent's hand. A good player is aware of this, and deliberately angles the hand in a misleading way before throwing down the symbol; for example, the player may rotate their wrist horizontally to give the impression that they plan to play paper, then turn it sideways at the last moment and play scissors instead. An experienced player looks at the opponent's whole body, not at the hands.

The kids I knew growing up who were really good at playing muk-ji-pa had quick nunchi, and this has clearly influenced what their lives are like now as adults. (Full disclosure: I refused to play.)

Notes

1. Kongdan Oh, "Korea's Path from Poverty to Philanthropy", Brookings Institute, 14 June 2010. https://www.brookings.edu/articles/koreas-path-from-poverty-to-philanthropy/

2. Minsoo Kang, *The Story of Hong Gildong* (New York: Penguin Books, 2016)

3. Jaehong Heo and Wonju Park, "Development and Validation of Nunchi Scale," *Korean Journal of Counseling* 14:6 (2013), pp. 3537–55

4. *Dumb and Dumber*, screenplay by Bobby and Peter Farrelly and Bennett Yellin (1994)

5. https://www.nytimes.com/1997/05/15/nyregion/danish-mother-is-reunited-with-her-baby.html

6. From his *Enchiridion*, which is Greek for 'manual'

7. "The Adventure of the Copper Beeches," Arthur Conan Doyle (1892)

8. https://www.pnas.org/content/115/7/E1690

9. Lee Soo-kyung, *The Fart with No Nunchi* (눈치 없는 방귀), illustrated by Lee Sang-yoon (Seoul: I&Book Publishing, 2015). I am

absolutely not making this up; here's proof: http://www.kyobobook
.co.kr/product/detailViewKor.laf?ejkGb=KOR&mallGb=
KOR&barcode=9791157920051&orderClick=LAG&Kc=

10. *The Office*, BBC, written by Ricky Gervais and Stephen Merchant

11. Walter Isaacson, *Steve Jobs* (New York: Simon & Schuster, 2011),
Chapter 30

12. https://www.reuters.com/sponsored/article/popularity-of
-gaming?

13. https://www.shortlist.com/entertainment/films/back-to-the
-future-wouldnt-have-been-the-same-without-spielberg/89788

14. https://www.sec.gov/news/press-release/2018-219

Acknowledgments

Acknowledgments usually say "This book could not have happened without editor so-and-so;" in this case, it's literally true on every level. Many thanks to Sarah Rigby, John Siciliano, and Pippa Wright at Penguin Random House, for being outstanding mentors, genius editors, and pleasant human beings. Props to Pamela Druckerman for helping introduce the word "nunchi" to Western audiences. A special nod to Pippa, for officiating this union of topic and author and for her unmatched literary instincts. John, my kindred spirit, secret weapon, and a breather of life into this project, has inspired me endlessly with his wit, nunchi-ful advice, and strategic thinking.

My agent Lizzy Kremer at David Higham Associates has been rounding out my jagged edges for fifteen years. I don't know what I did to deserve her, but having her in my corner has been one of the luckiest breaks of my life. Maddalena Cavaciuti and Harriet Moore share the devotion and finesse of their mentor, even though they were not given a choice about working with me, so thanks.

Thanks to Jai Ko, who provided valuable help with interviews.

As for personal thanks, there are far too many to name, but two people stand out: Siobhán Silke, whom I unbelievably forgot to mention last time, which is like forgetting my own name. She puts more energy into being a good person and friend than I have ever put into anything. And Kevin Klein, for being an ideal first reader, provider of wisdom, and purveyor of fine coffee.